编写委员会

总 主 编：郁云峰

副总主编：于天琪　陈维昌

主　　编：侯　伟

副 主 编：张　龙

编　　者：赵国宏　郑　冬　李亚博　张晓敏　马　琼　段望春
　　　　　别　威　石光岳　祁红梅　任耕田

编辑委员会

主　　任：陈维昌

副 主 任：付彦白

项目负责人：付彦白

项目秘书：武传霞

项目审定：王俊毅

项目成员：武传霞　王巧燕　方兴龙　赫　栗　张　彪

专家委员会（按音序排列）

陈曼倩	哈尔滨职业技术大学	崔永华	北京语言大学
梁赤民	中国-赞比亚职业技术学院	梁　宇	北京语言大学
刘建国	哈尔滨职业技术大学	宋继华	北京师范大学
宋　凯	有色金属工业人才中心	苏英霞	北京语言大学
赵丽霞	有色金属工业人才中心		

职通中文
Access to Vocational Chinese

增材制造技术应用

Application of Additive Manufacturing Technology

郁云峰 总主编
于天琪 陈维昌 副总主编
兰州资源环境职业技术大学 编

初级篇
Elementary

北京语言大学出版社
BEIJING LANGUAGE AND CULTURE
UNIVERSITY PRESS

© 2025 北京语言大学出版社，社图号 24180

图书在版编目（CIP）数据

增材制造技术应用 . 初级篇 / 郁云峰总主编；兰州资源环境职业技术大学编 . -- 北京：北京语言大学出版社，2025.8. --（"职通中文"系列教材）. -- ISBN 978-7-5619-6659-4

Ⅰ . H195.4

中国国家版本馆 CIP 数据核字第 2024UR4748 号

增材制造技术应用（初级篇）
ZENGCAI ZHIZAO JISHU YINGYONG (CHUJIPIAN)

责任编辑：	王巧燕　赫　栗
英文编辑：	侯晓娟
排版制作：	北京青侣文化创意设计有限公司
责任印制：	周　燚

出版发行：	北京语言大学出版社
社　　址：	北京市海淀区学院路 15 号，100083
网　　址：	www.blcup.com
电子信箱：	service@blcup.com
电　　话：	编辑部　　8610-82303647/3592/3395
	国内发行　8610-82303650/3591/3648
	海外发行　8610-82303365/3080/3668
	北语书店　8610-82303653
	网购咨询　8610-82303908
印　　刷：	北京瑞禾彩色印刷有限公司

版　　次：	2025 年 8 月第 1 版	印　　次：	2025 年 8 月第 1 次印刷
开　　本：	787 毫米 × 1092 毫米　1/16	印　　张：	23
字　　数：	267 千字		
定　　价：	115.00 元		

PRINTED IN CHINA

凡有印装质量问题，本社负责调换。售后QQ号1367565611，电话010-82303590

前言

为进一步推动各国学习者中文语言能力和专业技能深度融合，提升学习者围绕特定行业场景、典型工作任务使用中文进行沟通和交流的能力，持续满足中文学习者的职业规划和个人发展需求，实现优质教育资源共享，促进多彩文明交流互鉴，教育部中外语言交流合作中心联合有色金属工业人才中心，根据各国"中文+职业技能"教学发展实际需求，以中国职业院校为依托，组织职业教育、国际中文教育、出版和相关企业等领域的专家，共同研发"职通中文"系列教材及配套教学资源。

"职通中文"系列教材参照《国际中文教育中文水平等级标准》和《职业中文能力等级标准》，分为初、中、高三个等级。各等级均遵循"语言和技能相融合""好学、好教、好用"的编写理念，依据相关职业的典型工作场景、工作任务和高频用语，设计课文、会话、语言点和练习等板块，不断提升学习者在职业技术领域的中文应用水平和关键技术能力，为学习者尽快熟悉和适应工作环境提供帮助。本系列教材适用于在中国企业从事相关职业工作的各国员工，也适用于在华留学生或长短期培训人员，以及有意向了解中国语言文化和职业技能的学习者。

《增材制造技术应用（初级篇）》是"职通中文"系列教材之一，适用于增材制造领域的各国员工、学习者等人群。通过学习本教材，学习者能够用中文进行简单的工作交流，了解增材制造相关流程的操作技巧，读懂中文岗位说明书。

本教材在编写过程中，聘请行业专家、企业技术人员把关，调研驻外中国企业，了解企业对当地从业人员的语言、技能及总体素质的要求，将行业专家、企业一线从业人员认为学习者应该掌握的技能点作为内容选取的依据，精心挑选实际工作场景和典型工作任务中的真实语料，重构为符合"零基础"学习者水平的课文和对话。每个工作任务选取15个左右高频词语，以及工作中常用的短语和短句。全书共36课，每课包括复习、热身、学习生词、学习课文、学习语法、汉字书写、职业拓展/文化拓展和小结等八个部分，同时配有丰富的图片，力求以图文并茂的形式呈现真实的职业场景。此外，本教材还配套开发了音频、视频等资源，帮助学习者掌握在职业场景中用中文进行基本交际的能力。

学习者学习本教材后应当可以：

1. 具备基本的中文理解和运用能力，为职场应用和中文进阶学习打下基础；

2. 掌握增材制造工作中常用的基本词语、专业术语及常用表达，并将其应用到日常交际及工作岗位中；

3. 对中国文化具有基本的理解和认识，能够注意到与中国客户沟通交流时的文化差异，从而提升职业竞争力。

本教材得到了教育部中外语言交流合作中心、有色金属工业人才中心和专家组的支持，我们在此表示衷心感谢。本教材还得益于北京语言大学出版社的鼎力支持和精心指导，在此一并致谢。

"职通中文"系列教材的出版和应用能够促进各国"中文＋职业技能"人才的培养，推动当地经济发展，从而为构建人类命运共同体做出积极贡献。由于项目团队学识和相关经验有限，加之时间紧迫，本教材肯定有许多疏漏、不足之处。恳请本教材的使用者将发现的问题反馈给我们，以便再版和编写相关教材时改进。

编写团队
2024年11月

Preface

In order to further promote the deep integration of Chinese language proficiency and professional skills among learners from various countries and enhance their ability to communicate and interact in Chinese in specific industry scenarios and typical work tasks, the Center for Language Education and Cooperation under the Ministry of Education, in collaboration with China Nonferrous Metal Industry Talent Center, has organized experts from vocational education, international Chinese education, publishing, and related enterprises to jointly develop the "Access to Vocational Chinese" series of textbooks and supporting teaching resources. Based on the actual needs of "Chinese + Vocational Skills" teaching development in various countries and relying on Chinese vocational colleges, the series aims to continuously meet the career planning and personal development needs of Chinese learners, realize the sharing of high-quality educational resources, and promote exchanges and mutual learning among diverse civilizations.

In reference to *Chinese Proficiency Grading Standards for International Chinese Language Education* and *Chinese Proficiency Standards for Vocational Education*, the "Access to Vocational Chinese" series of textbooks is divided into three levels: elementary, intermediate, and advanced. All the levels follow the writing philosophy of "integrating language and skills" and "being easy to learn, teach, and use." The textbooks are designed around typical work scenarios, work tasks, and high-frequency terms of relevant professions, with sections on texts, conversations, language points, and exercises, continuously improving learners' Chinese application skills and key technical abilities in the vocational and technical fields, providing assistance for learners to quickly familiarize themselves with and adapt to the work environment. This series of textbooks is suitable for international employees engaged in relevant professions in Chinese companies, international students or trainees in China, as well as learners interested in Chinese language, culture, and vocational skills.

Application of Additive Manufacturing Technology (Elementary Level) is one of the textbooks in the "Access to Vocational Chinese" series, designed for employees, students, and others in the field of additive manufacturing. By studying this textbook, learners will be able to conduct simple work-related communication in Chinese, understand operational techniques related to additive manufacturing processes, and read Chinese job descriptions.

During the compilation of this textbook, industry experts and corporate technical personnel were consulted. Surveys were conducted in Chinese enterprises abroad to understand the language, skills, and overall quality requirements for local employees. The skills deemed essential by industry experts and frontline practitioners were used as the basis for content selection. Real-world work scenarios and typical tasks were carefully chosen, and authentic language materials were restructured into texts and dialogues suitable for learners without previous learning experience. Each work task includes around 15 high-frequency words, as well as commonly used phrases and short sentences. The textbook consists of 36 lessons, each including sections such as revision, warm-up, words and expressions, text, grammar, career/culture insight, and summary. Rich illustrations are provided to present realistic professional scenarios in a visually engaging manner. Additionally, the textbook is supplemented with audio and video resources to help learners master basic communication skills in professional settings using Chinese.

Preface

After completing this textbook, learners should be able to:

1. Have basic Chinese comprehension and application skills, laying the foundation for workplace use and further Chinese language learning.

2. Master commonly used basic words, professional terms, and expressions in additive manufacturing, and apply them in daily communication and job tasks.

3. Gain a basic understanding of Chinese culture, recognize cultural differences when communicating with Chinese clients, and enhance their professional competitiveness.

This textbook has received support from the Center for Language Education and Cooperation of the Ministry of Education of China, the Nonferrous Metals Industry Talent Center, and the expert team. We express our heartfelt gratitude to them. We also extend our thanks to Beijing Language and Culture University Press for their strong support and meticulous guidance.

The publication and application of the "Access to Vocational Chinese" series of textbooks aim to develop talents with "Chinese + Vocational Skills" across the globe, promote local economies, and make positive contributions to building a community with a shared future. Due to limited knowledge and related experience of the project team, as well as time constraints, this book is bound to have many deficiencies that need improvement. We sincerely invite users of this book to provide feedback on any issues discovered, so that we can make improvements in future editions and related materials.

Compiling team,
November 2024

词类简称表
List of Abbreviations of Parts of Speech

词性 Part of speech	英译 English	简称 Abbreviation
名词 míngcí	noun	*n.*
专有名词 zhuānyǒu míngcí	proper noun	*pn.*
代词 dàicí	pronoun	*pron.*
数词 shùcí	numeral	*num.*
量词 liàngcí	measure word	*m.*
数量词 shùliàngcí	quantifier	*q.*
动词 dòngcí	verb	*v.*
能愿动词 néngyuàn dòngcí	optative	*opt.*
形容词 xíngróngcí	adjective	*adj.*
副词 fùcí	adverb	*adv.*
介词 jiècí	preposition	*prep.*
连词 liáncí	conjunction	*conj.*
助词 zhùcí	particle	*part.*
叹词 tàncí	interjection	*int.*
前缀 qiánzhuì	prefix	*pref.*
后缀 hòuzhuì	suffix	*suf.*
短语 duǎnyǔ	phrase	*phr.*

目录 Contents

第 1 课	增材制造	Lesson 1	Additive Manufacturing	1
第 2 课	3D 建模	Lesson 2	3D Modeling	10
第 3 课	模型预处理	Lesson 3	Model Preprocessing	20
第 4 课	切片软件	Lesson 4	Slicing Software	30
第 5 课	模型打印	Lesson 5	Model Printing	40
第 6 课	模型后处理	Lesson 6	Model Postprocessing	51
第 7 课	三维扫描	Lesson 7	3D Scanning	60
第 8 课	逆向设计	Lesson 8	Reverse Design	69
第 9 课	熔融沉积成型	Lesson 9	Fused Deposition Modeling	78
第 10 课	光固化成型	Lesson 10	Stereolithography	87
第 11 课	激光成型	Lesson 11	Laser Forming	97
第 12 课	3D 打印机	Lesson 12	3D Printer	107
第 13 课	打印材料	Lesson 13	Printing Materials	116
第 14 课	识别激光器	Lesson 14	Identifying Lasers	125
第 15 课	操作水冷机	Lesson 15	Operating Water Chillers	134
第 16 课	添加原料	Lesson 16	Adding Raw Materials	144
第 17 课	操作软件	Lesson 17	Operating Software	154
第 18 课	检查设备	Lesson 18	Checking Equipment	164
第 19 课	启动设备	Lesson 19	Starting Equipment	174
第 20 课	操作设备	Lesson 20	Operating Equipment	185
第 21 课	添加支撑	Lesson 21	Adding Supports	195

第 22 课	预热基板	Lesson 22	Preheating the Substrate……205
第 23 课	操作激光器	Lesson 23	Operating Lasers……………215
第 24 课	测试光路	Lesson 24	Testing the Optical Path……225
第 25 课	设置参数	Lesson 25	Setting Parameters…………235
第 26 课	判断液位	Lesson 26	Judging Liquid Levels…………245
第 27 课	校准尺寸	Lesson 27	Calibrating Dimensions……255
第 28 课	多层制造	Lesson 28	Multi-layer Manufacturing……266
第 29 课	暂停和继续加工	Lesson 29	Pausing and Continuing Processing………………276
第 30 课	清洁机器	Lesson 30	Cleaning the Machine………286
第 31 课	检查机器	Lesson 31	Checking the Machine………296
第 32 课	调试机器	Lesson 32	Debugging the Machine……306
第 33 课	设备提示语	Lesson 33	Equipment Prompts…………316
第 34 课	注意安全	Lesson 34	Safety Precautions…………326
第 35 课	保养设备	Lesson 35	Equipment Maintenance……336
第 36 课	处理故障	Lesson 36	Troubleshooting……………346

第1课 Lesson 1

增材制造
Zēngcái zhìzào
Additive Manufacturing

 热身 Warm-up

你认识这些词语吗？ Do you know these words?

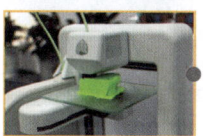

zhìzào 制造	—	manufacture
dǎyìn 打印	—	print
shùzì 数字	—	digit
móxíng 模型	—	model
jīqì 机器	—	machine
língjiàn 零件	—	part (of a machine)

学习生词 Words and Expressions 🎧 01-01

1	增材	zēngcái	*v.*	manufacture solid parts by the method of adding materials layer by layer
2	制造	zhìzào	*v.*	manufacture
3	知道	zhīdào	*v.*	know
4	技术	jìshù	*n.*	technology
5	打印	dǎyìn	*v.*	print
6	可以	kěyǐ	*opt.*	can
7	数字	shùzì	*n.*	digit
8	模型	móxíng	*n.*	model
9	成型	chéngxíng	*v.*	form, shape
10	在	zài	*prep.*	in, on, at
11	材料	cáiliào	*n.*	material
12	快速	kuàisù	*adj.*	quick
13	工业	gōngyè	*n.*	industry
14	产品	chǎnpǐn	*n.*	product
15	机器	jīqì	*n.*	machine
16	零件	língjiàn	*n.*	part (of a machine)

第 1 课 | 增材制造

词语练习 Word Exercises

1. 学习词语搭配。Study the collocations.

❶ zhìzào 制造	zhìzào chǎnpǐn 制造 产品	manufacture products
	zhìzào jīqì 制造 机器	manufacture machines
❷ dǎyìn 打印	dǎyìn chǎnpǐn 打印 产品	print products
	dǎyìn cáiliào 打印 材料	print materials
❸ chéngxíng 成型	kuàisù chéngxíng 快速 成型	rapid prototyping
	cáiliào chéngxíng 材料 成型	material forming

2. 给词语选择正确搭配。Choose the right words to form collocations.

❶ dǎyìn
　打印_____　　A. shùzì 数字　　B. chǎnpǐn 产品

❷ _____chéngxíng 成型　　A. cáiliào 材料　　B. jìshù 技术

❸ zhìzào
　制造_____　　A. jīqì 机器　　B. chéngxíng 成型

3

学习课文 Text 🎧 01-02

Q：你知道增材制造技术吗？

A：我知道。

Q：增材制造技术是3D打印吗？

A：是的，它可以把数字模型打印成型。

Q：它可以用在材料快速成型上吗？

A：可以。

Q：3D打印可以做什么？

A：可以制造工业产品、机器零件。

Q: Do you know additive manufacturing technology?

A: Yes, I do.

Q: Is additive manufacturing technology the same as 3D printing?

第 1 课 | 增材制造

A: Yes, it can print digital models into physical forms.

Q: Can it be used for rapid material prototyping?

A: Yes, it can.

Q: What can 3D printing do?

A: It can manufacture industrial products and machine parts.

课文练习 Text Exercises

1. 回答问题。Answer the questions.

① 增材制造技术是 3D 打印吗？

② 增材制造可以用在工业产品制造吗？

2. 根据课文选词填空。Choose the words to fill in the blanks based on the text.

| A. 成型 | B. 知道 | C. 快速 | D. 可以 |

① 我_____。

② 增材制造_____用在工业产品制造上。

学习语法 Grammar

语法点 1　Grammar Point 1

能愿动词"可以"　The optative verb "可以"

It means "can" or "may". Its negative form is "不能".

1. 可以用 3D 打印制造产品吗？
2. 增材制造技术可以制造工业产品。
3. 你可以再读一遍吗？

给"可以"选择正确的位置。Choose the right positions for " 可以 ".

1. A 用 B 增材制造 C 产品吗？　　　　　　　　　　(　　)
2. A 增材制造技术 B 制造 C 工业产品。　　　　　　(　　)
3. A 你 B 再读 C 一遍吗？　　　　　　　　　　　　(　　)
4. A 你们 B 大声 C 读课文吗？　　　　　　　　　　(　　)

语法点 2　Grammar Point 2

介词"在"　The preposition "在"

It is used to introduce the location or scope of an action or behavior. The common structures are: 在 + nominal phrase + verbal phrase; verbal phrase + 在 + nominal phrase.

第1课 | 增材制造

1. 3D打印制造的零件可以用在机器上吗？
2. 增材制造技术可以用在工业上。
3. 在工业上，增材制造技术可以做什么？

给"在"选择正确的位置。Choose the right positions for "在".

1. A 增材制造技术 B 可以用 C 工业制造上。　　　　　（　　）
2. A 增材制造技术可以 B 用 C 材料快速成型上吗？　　（　　）
3. A 工业上，3D打印 B 可以 C 做什么？　　　　　　　（　　）
4. A 增材制造技术 B 可以用 C 零件制造上吗？　　　　（　　）

 汉字书写 Writing Chinese Characters

wén
文 文 文 文 文
文 文 文 文 文

kě
可 可 可 可 可
可 可 可 可 可

yī
一 一 一 一 一
一 一 一 一 一

shǎo
少 少 少 少 少
少 少 少 少 少

文化拓展 Culture Insight

Chinese New Year, also known as Spring Festival, stands as one of the most significant and distinctive traditional festivals celebrated by the Chinese people. It typically encompasses the Chinese New Year's Eve and the first day of the first lunar month. Marking the commencement of the year, it is colloquially referred to as "Guonian" in Chinese. The festivities begin from "Laba", which falls on the eighth day of the twelfth lunar month, or from "Xiaonian" (Little Chinese New Year 23rd day of the twelfth lunar month in northern China, and 24th day in southern China), and continue until the Lantern Festival. In honor of the Chinese New Year, a myriad of culturally rich activities is undertaken, including venerating ancestors, honoring the elderly, expressing gratitude and bestowing blessings, reuniting with family, discarding the old to welcome the new, ushering in good fortune, and offering prayers for a bountiful year ahead.

小结 Summary

1. 听句子选词填空。Listen to the sentences and choose the words to fill in the blanks. 🎧 01-03

| A. 成型 | B. 快速 | C. 技术 | D. 知道 |

❶ 增材制造_____是3D打印吗？

2 它可以把数字模型打印_____。

3 它可以把材料_____成型吗?

4 你_____增材制造技术吗?

2. 看词语练拼音。Look at the words and practice Pinyin.

| gōngyè | shùzì | móxíng | dǎyìn |
| 工业 | 数字 | 模型 | 打印 |

| jìshù | kuàisù | língjiàn | cáiliào |
| 技术 | 快速 | 零件 | 材料 |

3. 朗读下列句子。Read aloud the following sentences.

1 Tā kěyǐ bǎ shùzì móxíng dǎyìn chéngxíng.
它可以把数字模型打印成型。

2 Kěyǐ zhìzào gōngyè chǎnpǐn、jīqì língjiàn.
可以制造工业产品、机器零件。

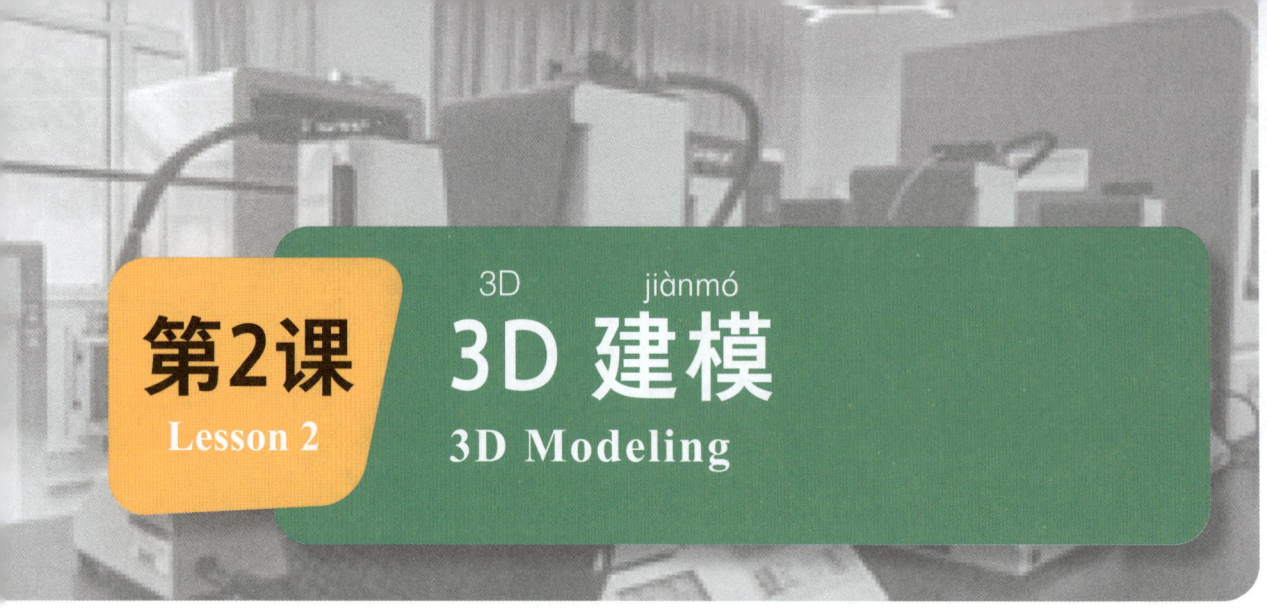

第2课 Lesson 2

3D 建模
3D Modeling

 复习 Revision

1. 根据图片选择词语。Choose the words based on the pictures.

① 材料（　　）　　② 打印（　　）　　③ 制造（　　）
　 模型（　　）　　　 技术（　　）　　　 数字（　　）

2. 把下列词语组合成短语或句子。Connect the words into phrases or sentences.

① ①你　②吗　③增材制造　④知道

_____

② ①模型　②打印　③数字　④成型

_____

第2课 | 3D建模

 ①产品   ②工业   ③制造   ④可以

_____

热身 Warm-up

你认识这些词语吗？ Do you know these words?

- 软件 ruǎnjiàn — software
- 界面 jièmiàn — interface
- 文件 wénjiàn — file
- 绘制 huìzhì — draw
- 三维 sānwéi — 3D (three-dimensional)
- 图形 túxíng — graphic

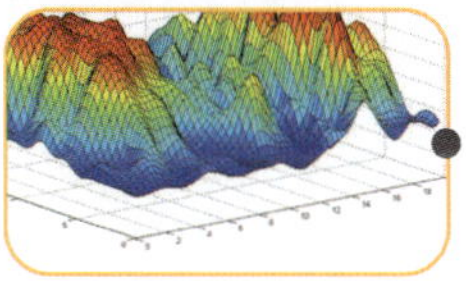

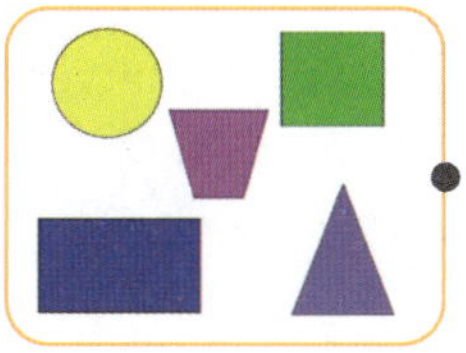

11

 学习生词 **Words and Expressions** 🎧 02-01

1	建模	jiànmó	v.	model
2	软件	ruǎnjiàn	n.	software
3	会	huì	opt.	can, know how to
4	打开	dǎ//kāi	v.	open
5	界面	jièmiàn	n.	interface
6	选择	xuǎnzé	v.	choose
7	哪个	nǎge	pron.	which
8	模块	mókuài	n.	module
9	创建	chuàngjiàn	v.	create
10	文件	wénjiàn	n.	file
11	图形	túxíng	n.	graphic
12	绘制	huìzhì	v.	draw
13	三维	sānwéi	adj.	3D (three-dimensional)
14	对	duì	adj.	correct
15	保存	bǎocún	v.	save

第 2 课 | 3D 建模

词语练习 Word Exercises

1. 学习词语搭配。Study the collocations.

❶ chuàngjiàn 创建	chuàngjiàn wénjiàn 创建 文件	create a file
	chuàngjiàn móxíng 创建 模型	create a model
❷ dǎkāi 打开	dǎkāi ruǎnjiàn 打开 软件	open the software
	dǎkāi wénjiàn 打开 文件	open a file
❸ bǎocún 保存	bǎocún ruǎnjiàn 保存 软件	save the software
	bǎocún wénjiàn 保存 文件	save a file

2. 给词语选择正确搭配。Choose the right words to form collocations.

❶ huìzhì
绘制_____　　A. jìshù 技术　　B. túxíng 图形

❷ dǎkāi
打开_____　　A. ruǎnjiàn 软件　　B. duì de 对的

❸ bǎocún
保存_____　　A. xuǎnzé 选择　　B. wénjiàn 文件

学习课文 Text 🎧 02-02

课文1 建模软件
Kèwén 1　Jiànmó ruǎnjiàn

Q：你会打开软件吗？
　　Nǐ huì dǎkāi ruǎnjiàn ma?

A：我会。
　　Wǒ huì.

Q：你会打开UG软件的界面吗？
　　Nǐ huì dǎkāi UG ruǎnjiàn de jièmiàn ma?

A：我会。
　　Wǒ huì.

Q：选择哪个模块？
　　Xuǎnzé nǎge mókuài?

A：选择"创建文件"。
　　Xuǎnzé "chuàngjiàn wénjiàn".

Text 1　Modeling Software

Q: Can you open the software?

A: Yes, I can.

Q: Can you open the interface of the UG software?

A: Yes, I can.

Q: Which module will you choose?

A: I'll choose "Create a file".

第 2 课 | 3D 建模

课文 2　图形绘制
Kèwén 2　Túxíng huìzhì

Q： 你 绘制 的 三维 图形 对 吗？
　　Nǐ huìzhì de sānwéi túxíng duì ma?

A： 对。
　　Duì.

Q： 你 保存 建模 文件 了 吗？
　　Nǐ bǎocún jiànmó wénjiàn le ma?

A： 我 保存 了。
　　Wǒ bǎocún le.

Text 2　Graphic Drawing

Q: Is the 3D graphic that I drew correct?

A: Yes.

Q: Did you save the modeling file?

A: Yes, I did.

课文练习　Text Exercises

1. 回答问题。Answer the questions.

   ① 你会打开软件吗？

   ② 你保存建模文件了吗？

2. 根据课文选词填空。Choose the words to fill in the blanks based on the text.

> A. 可以　　　B. 对　　　C. 知道　　　D. 会

1 我绘制的三维图形_____吗？

2 你_____打开 UG 软件的界面吗？

学习语法 Grammar

语法点 1　Grammar Point 1

能愿动词"会"　The optative verb "会"

It means a skill acquired through learning.

1 你会打开软件吗？

2 我会保存建模文件。

3 我会创建文件。

连词成句。Connect the words into phrases or sentences.

1 打开　我　会　软件

_____

2 你　会　保存　建模　文件　吗

_____

3 会 文件 吗 你 创建

_____

4 说 我们 会 中文

_____

语法点 2　Grammar Point 2

语气助词"了"　The modal particle "了"

It is used after a verb to indicate the completion of an action. The common structure is: verb + object + 了, and the negative structure is: 没(有) + verb + object.

1 你保存建模文件了吗?

2 我打开文件了。

3 我打开软件了。

连词成句。Connect the words into phrases or sentences.

1 建模　我　文件　保存　了

_____

2 保存　文件　我　了

_____

3 软件　了　吗　你　打开

_____

4 发音　练习　了　你　吗

_____

 汉字书写 Writing Chinese Characters

kāi 开 开 开 开
开 开 开 开 开

guān 关 关 关 关 关 关
关 关 关 关 关

zhōng 中 中 中 中
中 中 中 中 中

xīn 心 心 心 心
心 心 心 心 心

 职业拓展 Career Insight

The mid-1990s marked the advent of additive manufacturing, a technology whose operational principles closely resemble those of conventional printing. Utilizing computer-controlled machinery, it rapidly deposits "printing materials" layer by layer, transforming digital model files into tangible objects. This innovative process has also earned it the name 3D stereoscopic printing.

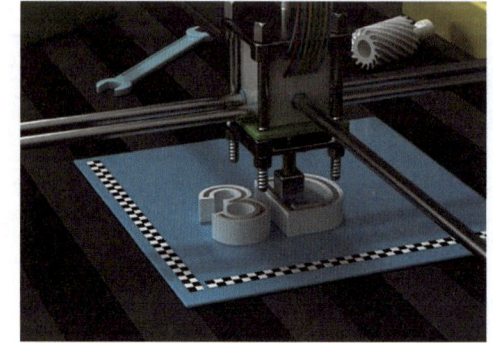

第 2 课 | 3D 建模

 小结 Summary

1. 听句子选词填空。Listen to the sentences and choose the words to fill in the blanks. 🎧 02-03

| A. 建模　　B. 三维　　C. 打开　　D. 创建 |

① 你会_____UG 软件的界面吗？

② 选择"_____文件"。

③ 我绘制的_____图形对吗？

④ 你保存_____文件了吗？

2. 看词语练拼音。Look at the words and practice Pinyin.

xuǎnzé　　chuàngjiàn　　jiànmó　　huì
选择　　　创建　　　　建模　　会

nǎge　　jièmiàn　　bǎocún　　dǎkāi
哪个　　界面　　　保存　　　打开

3. 朗读下列句子。Read aloud the following sentences.

Xuǎnzé nǎge mókuài?
① 选择 哪个 模块？

Nǐ bǎocún jiànmó wénjiàn le ma?
② 你 保存 建模 文件 了 吗？

19

第3课 Lesson 3

Móxíng yùchǔlǐ
模型预处理
Model Preprocessing

 复习 Revision

1. 根据图片选择词语。Choose the words based on the pictures.

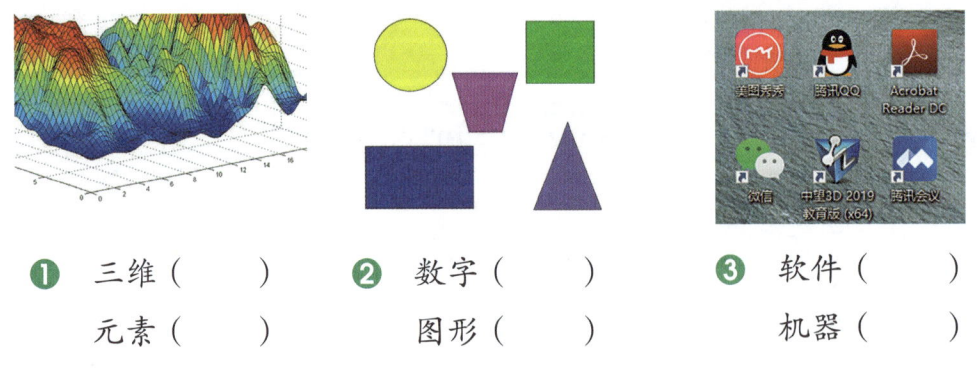

❶ 三维（   ）   ❷ 数字（   ）   ❸ 软件（   ）
　 元素（   ）   　 图形（   ）   　 机器（   ）

2. 连词成句。Connect the words into sentences.

❶ ①会　　②软件　　③打开　　④你　　⑤吗

_____

❷ ①哪个　　②模块　　③选择　　④你

_____

第3课 | 模型预处理

3 ①保存　②请　③建模　④文件

热身 Warm-up

你认识这些词语吗？ Do you know these words?

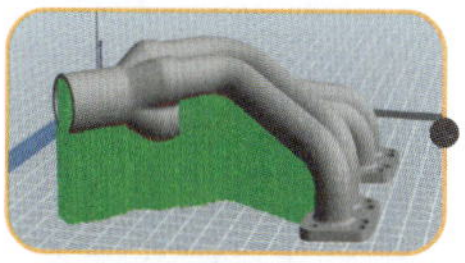

zhīchēng 支撑	support
tiānjiā 添加	add
biànxíng 变形	deform
fēncéng 分层	be layered
qiēpiàn 切片	slice
xiāngděng 相等	be equal

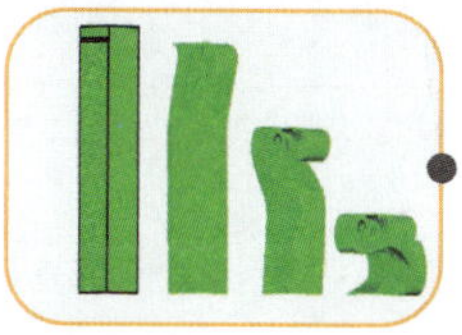

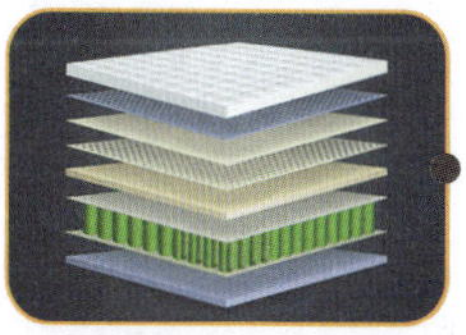

21

学习生词 Words and Expressions 03-01

1	预处理	yùchǔlǐ	v.	preprocess
2	添加	tiānjiā	v.	add
3	支撑	zhīchēng	v.	support
4	需要	xūyào	opt.	need
5	为什么	wèi shénme	phr.	why
6	防止	fángzhǐ	v.	prevent
7	变形	biànxíng	v.	deform
8	分层	fēncéng	v.	be layered
9	切片	qiēpiàn	v.	slice
10	什么	shénme	pron.	what
11	生成	shēngchéng	v.	generate
12	厚度	hòudù	n.	thickness
13	相等	xiāngděng	v.	be equal
14	影响	yǐngxiǎng	v.	influence, affect
15	精度	jīngdù	n.	accuracy

第 3 课 | 模型预处理

 词语练习 Word Exercises

1. 学习词语搭配。Study the collocations.

❶ tiānjiā 添加	tiānjiā zhīchēng 添加 支撑	add support
	tiānjiā cáiliào 添加 材料	add materials
❷ shēngchéng 生成	shēngchéng wénjiàn 生成 文件	generate files
	shēngchéng móxíng 生成 模型	generate a model
❸ yǐngxiǎng 影响	yǐngxiǎng jīngdù 影响 精度	impact accuracy
	yǐngxiǎng chéngxíng 影响 成型	impact molding

2. 给词语选择正确搭配。Choose the right words to form collocations.

❶ _____预处理(yùchǔlǐ)　A. 文件(wénjiàn)　B. 模型(móxíng)

❷ 分层(fēncéng)_____　A. 切片(qiēpiàn)　B. 界面(jièmiàn)

❸ 厚度(hòudù)_____　A. 可以(kěyǐ)　B. 相等(xiāngděng)

23

 学习课文 Text 🎧 03-02

课文 1 添加支撑
Kèwén 1 Tiānjiā zhīchēng

Q: 模型 需要 添加 支撑 吗?
   Móxíng xūyào tiānjiā zhīchēng ma?

A: 对,需要。
   Duì, xūyào.

Q: 为什么?
   Wèi shénme?

A: 防止 模型 打印 变形。
   Fángzhǐ móxíng dǎyìn biànxíng.

Text 1   Adding Support

Q: Does the model need support?

A: Yes, it does.

Q: Why?

A: To prevent model deformation during printing.

第 3 课 | 模型预处理

课文 2 分层切片
Kèwén 2 Fēncéng qiēpiàn

Q：什么是分层切片？
　　Shénme shì fēncéng qiēpiàn?

A：把模型生成厚度相等的多层模型。
　　Bǎ móxíng shēngchéng hòudù xiāngděng de duōcéng móxíng.

Q：有什么影响？
　　Yǒu shénme yǐngxiǎng?

A：分层厚度影响打印的精度。
　　Fēncéng hòudù yǐngxiǎng dǎyìn de jīngdù.

Text 2　Layered Slicing

Q: What is layered slicing?
A: It generates multiple layers of the model with equal thickness.
Q: What is the impact?
A: The layer thickness affects the printing accuracy.

课文练习 Text Exercises

1. 回答问题。Answer the questions.

① 模型打印需要添加支撑吗？

② 模型打印需要分层切片吗？

2. 根据课文选词填空。Choose the words to fill in the blanks based on the text.

> A. 精度　　　B. 什么　　　C. 生成　　　D. 防止

① 把模型_____厚度相等的多层模型。

② 分层厚度影响打印的_____。

 学习语法 Grammar

语法点 1　Grammar Point 1

"把"字句　"把" sentences

It means to change the position or state of a person or thing by means of an action or behavior. The basic structure is: subject + "把" + object + verbal phrase.

① 把 3D 模型生成厚度相等的多层模型。

② 把软件打开。

③ 我把建模文件保存了。

连词成句。Connect the words into sentences.

① 把　　多层　　模型　　生成　　模型

_____

2 软件　把　打开

_____

3 文件　把　了　保存　我

_____

4 材料　快速　把　成型

_____

语法点 2　Grammar Point 2

> **结构助词"的"　The structural particle "的"**
>
> The particle "的" is used to connect an attribute and a central noun. The common structure is: attribute + "的" + central noun.
>
> 1 把 3D 模型生成厚度相等的多层模型。
> 2 分层厚度影响打印的精度。
> 3 你会打开软件的界面吗?

给"的"选择正确的位置。Choose the right positions for "的".

1 多层模型 A 厚度 B 相等 C 吗?　　　　　　　　　　(　　)

2 分层 A 厚度 B 影响打印 C 精度。　　　　　　　　　(　　)

3 这 A 是 B 你 C 中文书吗?　　　　　　　　　　　　(　　)

4 我 A 是 B 你们 C 老师。　　　　　　　　　　　　　(　　)

 汉字书写 Writing Chinese Characters

 文化拓展 Culture Insight

Ceramics, encompassing both pottery and porcelain, represent a significant category of Chinese handicrafts. Dating back to the Neolithic Age, China has been renowned for its production of colored and black pottery, characterized by their rustic and unadorned aesthetic. Pottery and porcelain differ fundamentally in their textures and properties. Pottery is primarily crafted from clay that is highly viscous and plastic, whereas porcelain is made from a blend of clay,

feldspar, and quartz. Traditional Chinese ceramic crafts are celebrated for their superior quality and exquisite appearance, holding considerable artistic value and enjoying global acclaim.

小结 Summary

1. 听句子选词填空。**Listen to the sentences and choose the words to fill in the blanks.** 🎧 03-03

> A. 变形　　　B. 分层　　　C. 影响　　　D. 需要

① 模型_____添加支撑吗？

② 防止模型打印_____。

③ 什么是_____切片？

④ 分层厚度_____打印的精度。

2. 看词语练拼音。**Look at the words and practice Pinyin.**

| wèi shénme | hòudù | biànxíng | zhīchēng |
| 为 什么 | 厚度 | 变形 | 支撑 |

| yǐngxiǎng | fēncéng | jīngdù | yùchǔlǐ |
| 影响 | 分层 | 精度 | 预处理 |

3. 朗读下列句子。**Read aloud the following sentences.**

① Móxíng xūyào tiānjiā zhīchēng ma?
　模型 需要 添加 支撑 吗？

② Bǎ móxíng shēngchéng hòudù xiāngděng de duōcéng móxíng.
　把 模型 生成 厚度 相等 的 多层 模型。

第4课 Lesson 4
切片软件 Qiēpiàn ruǎnjiàn
Slicing Software

 复习 Revision

1. 根据图片选择词语。Choose the words based on the pictures.

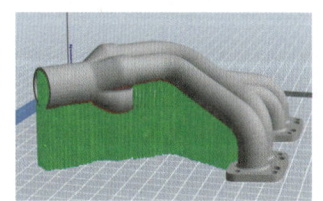      

❶ 模块（   ）　　❷ 相等（   ）　　❸ 选择（   ）
　 支撑（   ）　　　 哪个（   ）　　　 切片（   ）

2. 把下列词语组合成短语或句子。Connect the words into phrases or sentences.

1 ①打印　②模型　③变形　④防止

_____

2 ①需要　②添加　③模型　④支撑

_____

第4课 | 切片软件

3 ①分层   ②影响   ③厚度   ④精度

_____

热身 Warm-up

你认识这些词语吗？ Do you know these words?

📄	dǎorù 导入	import
📱 参数表	cānshù 参数	parameter
🗺️	wèizhì 位置	position
🚗	zìdòng 自动	automatic
🔧	bìhòu 壁厚	wall thickness
📱	wàiké 外壳	shell

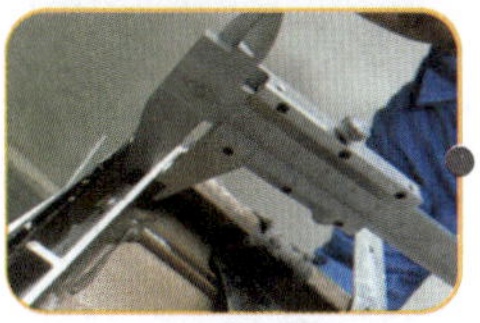

学习生词 Words and Expressions  04-01

1	导入	dǎorù	v.	import
2	设定	shèdìng	v.	set
3	参数	cānshù	n.	parameter
4	合理	hélǐ	adj.	reasonable
5	摆放	bǎifàng	v.	put, place
6	位置	wèizhì	n.	position
7	完成	wán//chéng	v.	finish, complete
8	自动	zìdòng	adj.	automatic
9	时候	shíhou	n.	(a point in) time
10	层厚	cénghòu	n.	layer thickness
11	和	hé	conj.	and
12	壁厚	bìhòu	n.	wall thickness
13	决定	juédìng	v.	determine
14	质量	zhìliàng	n.	quality
15	外壳	wàiké	n.	shell

词语练习 Word Exercises

1. 学习词语搭配。Study the collocations.

① dǎorù 导入	dǎorù wénjiàn 导入 文件	import a file
	dǎorù cānshù 导入 参数	import parameters
② wánchéng 完成	dǎyìn wánchéng 打印 完成	printing is completed
	chuàngjiàn wánchéng 创建 完成	creation is completed
③ zìdòng 自动	zìdòng dǎyìn 自动 打印	automatic printing
	zìdòng dǎkāi 自动 打开	automatic opening

2. 给词语选择正确搭配。Choose the right words to form collocations.

① bǎifàng
　摆放_____　　A. cénghòu 层厚　　B. wèizhì 位置

② shèdìng
　设定_____　　A. cānshù 参数　　B. túxíng 图形

③ juédìng
　决定_____　　A. zhìliàng 质量　　B. jiànmó 建模

学习课文 Text 🎧 04-02

课文 1　软件 切片
Kèwén 1　Ruǎnjiàn qiēpiàn

第一步： 把模型导入软件。
Dì-yī bù: Bǎ móxíng dǎorù ruǎnjiàn.

第二步： 设定参数。
Dì-èr bù: Shèdìng cānshù.

第三步： 选择合理摆放位置。
Dì-sān bù: Xuǎnzé hélǐ bǎifàng wèizhì.

第四步： 完成软件自动切片。
Dì-sì bù: Wánchéng ruǎnjiàn zìdòng qiēpiàn.

Text 1　Slicing by the Software

Step 1: Import the model into the software.

Step 2: Set the parameters.

Step 3: Choose a reasonable position for placement.

Step 4: The software automatically completes the slicing.

课文 2 参数 设定
Kèwén 2 Cānshù shèdìng

Q: 切片的时候，设定什么参数？
Qiēpiàn de shíhou, shèdìng shénme cānshù?

A: 设定层厚和壁厚。
Shèdìng cénghòu hé bìhòu.

Q: 什么是层厚？
Shénme shì cénghòu?

A: 它是切片厚度，层厚决定打印质量。
Tā shì qiēpiàn hòudù, cénghòu juédìng dǎyìn zhìliàng.

Q: 什么是壁厚？
Shénme shì bìhòu?

A: 它是模型外壳厚度。
Tā shì móxíng wàiké hòudù.

Text 2 Parameter Setting

Q: What parameters should be set when slicing?

A: Layer thickness and wall thickness.

Q: What is layer thickness?

A: It's the thickness of each slice and determines the print quality.

Q: What is wall thickness?

A: It is the thickness of the model's shell.

课文练习 Text Exercises

1. 回答问题。 Answer the questions.

① 切片的时候，设定什么参数？

② 层厚决定打印质量吗？

2. 根据课文选词填空。 Choose the words to fill in the blanks based on the text.

| A. 合理 | B. 自动 | C. 质量 | D. 壁厚 |

① _____是模型外壳厚度。

② 选择_____摆放位置。

学习语法 Grammar

 语法点 1 Grammar Point 1

……的时候 "(when)..."

The phrase "……的时候" can alternatively be expressed as "当……的时候". It indicates "at a specific time point or during a particular period of time" and functions as an adverbial modifier in a sentence. In written Chinese, "……时" is often used.

① 切片的时候，设定什么参数？

② 打印的时候，需要选择层厚。

③ 打印的时候，需要选择壁厚。

给"的时候"选择正确的位置。Choose the right positions for "的时候".

1️⃣ A 切片 B，C 设定什么参数？　　　　　　　　　　（　　）

2️⃣ A 打印模型 B，C 需要添加支撑。　　　　　　　　（　　）

3️⃣ A 保存文件 B，C 需要选择什么模块？　　　　　　（　　）

4️⃣ A 打印 B，需要选择层厚。　　　　　　　　　　　（　　）

语法点 2　Grammar Point 2

> **连词"和"**　The conjunction "和"
>
> It indicates a joint relationship and is often used to connect two or more nominal components.

1️⃣ 设定层厚和壁厚。

2️⃣ 增材制造技术可以制造工业产品和机器零件。

3️⃣ 我们练习生词和发音。

选词填空。Choose the words to fill in the blanks.

> A. 在　　　　B. 和

1️⃣ 增材制造技术可以用＿＿＿＿零件制造上吗？

2️⃣ 需要设定层厚＿＿＿＿壁厚。

3️⃣ ＿＿＿＿工业产品上，3D 打印可以做什么？

4️⃣ 我会打开软件＿＿＿＿保存文件。

 汉字书写 Writing Chinese Characters

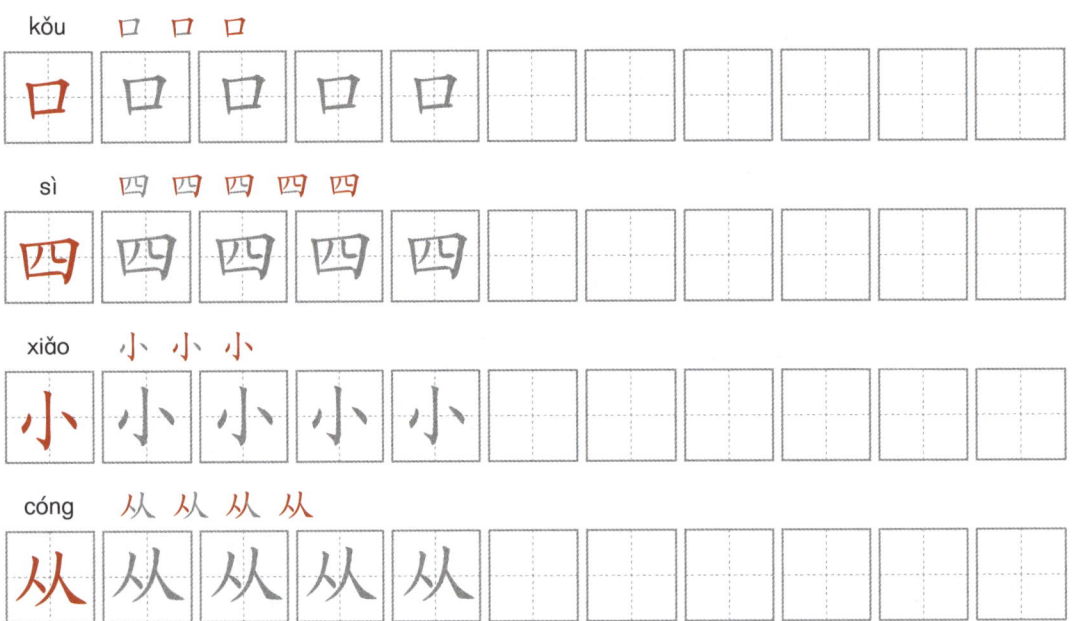

 职业拓展 Career Insight

The function of slicing software is to divide a complete 3D model into numerous layers. Professionally, it plans the path for the printer's XYZ axes and the extrusion amount for the extruder, and saves these instructions as a file format recognizable by the printer.

第 4 课 | 切片软件

 **小结 Summary**

1. 听句子选词填空。Listen to the sentences and choose the words to fill in the blanks. 🎧 04-03

   > A. 设定　　　B. 质量　　　C. 自动　　　D. 和

   ① 设定层厚_____壁厚。

   ② 完成软件_____切片。

   ③ 切片的时候，_____什么参数？

   ④ 层厚决定打印_____。

2. 看词语练拼音。Look at the words and practice Pinyin.

cānshù	shèdìng	zìdòng	wèizhì
参数	设定	自动	位置
bǎifàng	juédìng	zhìliàng	wàiké
摆放	决定	质量	外壳

3. 朗读下列句子。Read aloud the following sentences.

   ① Qiēpiàn de shíhou, shèdìng shénme cānshù?
   切片 的 时候，设定 什么 参数？

   ② Tā shì qiēpiàn hòudù, cénghòu juédìng dǎyìn zhìliàng.
   它 是 切片 厚度，层厚 决定 打印 质量。

39

第5课 Lesson 5
模型打印 Móxíng dǎyìn
Model Printing

 复习 Revision

1. 根据图片选择词语。Choose the words based on the pictures.

  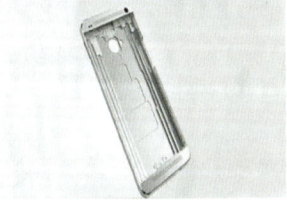

❶ 生成（　　）　　❷ 自动（　　）　　❸ 零件（　　）
　 位置（　　）　　　 打开（　　）　　　 外壳（　　）

2. 把下列词语组合成短语或句子。Connect the words into phrases or sentences.

① ①模型　②软件　③导入　④把

_____

② ①摆放　②选择　③合理　④位置

_____

第5课 | 模型打印

 ①打印　②决定　③层厚　④质量

_____

热身 Warm-up

你认识这些词语吗？ Do you know these words?

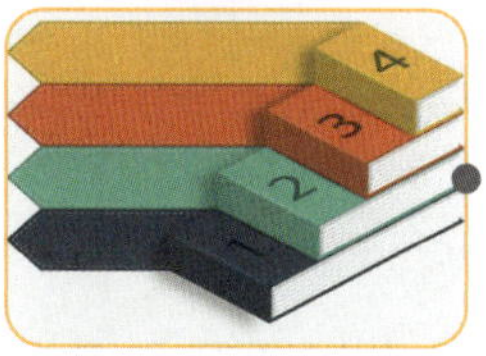

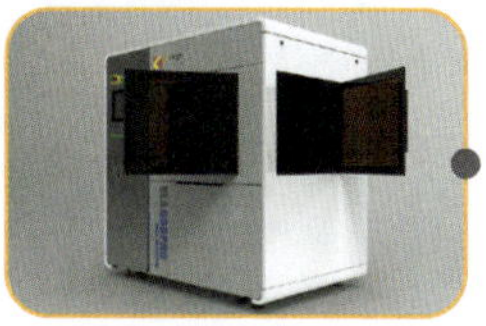

电脑图片	diànnǎo 电脑	computer
步骤图片	bùzhòu 步骤	step
DBF→Excel图片	zhuǎnhuàn 转换	convert
文件格式icon	géshi 格式	format
修复前后图片	xiūfù 修复	repair
设备图片	shèbèi 设备	equipment

41

学习生词 Words and Expressions  05-01

1	处理	chǔlǐ	v.	process, handle
2	控制	kòngzhì	v.	control
3	电脑	diànnǎo	n.	computer
4	前	qián	n.	(the time) before
5	进行	jìnxíng	v.	perform, conduct
6	转换	zhuǎnhuàn	v.	convert
7	步骤	bùzhòu	n.	step
8	成	chéng	v.	become, turn into
9	格式	géshi	n.	format
10	检查	jiǎnchá	v.	check
11	并	bìng	conj.	and
12	修复	xiūfù	v.	repair
13	准备	zhǔnbèi	v.	prepare
14	开启	kāiqǐ	v.	start, turn on
15	设备	shèbèi	n.	equipment

第 5 课 | 模型打印

词语练习 Word Exercises

1. 学习词语搭配。Study the collocations.

kòngzhì 控制	kòngzhì diànnǎo 控制 电脑	control the computer
	kòngzhì shèbèi 控制 设备	control the equipment
jiǎnchá 检查	jiǎnchá wénjiàn 检查 文件	check the file
	jiǎnchá shèbèi 检查 设备	check the equipment
xiūfù 修复	xiūfù chǎnpǐn 修复 产品	repair the product
	xiūfù jīqì 修复 机器	repair the machine

2. 给词语选择正确搭配。Choose the right words to form collocations.

① jìnxíng 进行_____   A. sānwéi 三维   B. yùchǔlǐ 预处理

② zhǔnbèi 准备_____   A. géshi 格式   B. dǎyìn 打印

③ kāiqǐ 开启_____   A. shèbèi 设备   B. bùzhòu 步骤

学习课文 Text 🎧 05-02

课文 1 文件处理

Q：把文件导入控制电脑前，需要进行预处理吗？

A：需要。

Q：文件格式需要转换吗？

A：需要。

Text 1 File Processing

Q: Is file preprocessing necessary before importing the file into the control computer?

A: Yes, it is.

Q: Does the file format need to be converted?

A: Yes, it does.

课文 2　打印步骤
Kèwén 2　Dǎyìn bùzhòu

第一步：转换成 STL 格式。
Dì-yī bù: Zhuǎnhuàn chéng STL géshi.

第二步：检查并修复文件。
Dì-èr bù: Jiǎnchá bìng xiūfù wénjiàn.

第三步：对模型进行切片并添加支撑。
Dì-sān bù: Duì móxíng jìnxíng qiēpiàn bìng tiānjiā zhīchēng.

第四步：准备打印材料。
Dì-sì bù: Zhǔnbèi dǎyìn cáiliào.

第五步：开启设备，打印模型。
Dì-wǔ bù: Kāiqǐ shèbèi, dǎyìn móxíng.

Text 2　Printing Steps

Step 1: Convert it to the STL format.

Step 2: Check and repair the file.

Step 3: Slice the model and add supports.

Step 4: Prepare the printing materials.

Step 5: Turn on the equipment and print the model.

课文练习 Text Exercises

1. 回答问题。 Answer the questions.

① 模型文件需要进行格式转换吗?

② 需要对模型进行切片并添加支撑吗?

2. 根据课文选词填空。 Choose the words to fill in the blanks based on the text.

| A. 开启 | B. 进行 | C. 处理 | D. 转换 |

① 模型文件需要_____为 STL 格式。

② _____打印设备,打印产品。

学习语法 Grammar

语法点 1　Grammar Point 1

介词 "对"　The preposition "对"

It is used to introduce the object involved in an action. The common structure is: 对 + noun + verbal phrase.

① 对模型文件进行预处理。

② 对模型进行软件切片。

③ 对文件格式进行转换。

选词填空。Choose the words to fill in the blanks.

A. 对 B. 在

1 _____ 模型文件进行预处理。

2 _____ 工业上，3D 打印可以做什么？

3 _____ 文件格式进行转换。

4 你把文件保存_____哪儿了？

语法点 2 Grammar Point 2

连词"并" The conjunction "并"

It is used to connect juxtaposed verbs or adjectives, indicating that several actions are performed simultaneously or several properties exist simultaneously. It can also be expressed as "并且".

1 检查并修复 STL 文件。

2 对模型进行软件切片并添加支撑。

3 打开工作界面并创建文件。

用"并"改写下列句子。Rewrite the following sentences with "并".

1 检查 STL 文件，修复 STL 文件。

_____

2 对模型进行软件切片，添加支撑。

_____

3 打开工作界面,选择"创建文件"。

_____

4 打开软件,设定参数。

_____

 汉字书写 Writing Chinese Characters

 ## 文化拓展 Culture Insight

The Great Wall, often referred to as the Ten Thousand *Li* Great Wall, stands as an ancient military defense fortification in China. It is characterized by its towering, robust, and continuous structure, designed to impede the advance of enemy cavalry. Distinct from a solitary city wall, the Great Wall constitutes a comprehensive defense system centered around city walls, enhanced by numerous towns, barriers, pavilions, and landmarks. Over 43,000 related facilities of the Great Wall cultural relics remain today. In December 1987, the Great Wall was inscribed as a World Heritage Site.

 ## 小结 Summary

1. 听句子选词填空。Listen to the sentences and choose the words to fill in the blanks. 05-03

   A. 准备   B. 控制   C. 并   D. 转换

   ① 把文件导入_____电脑。   ② 文件格式需要_____吗？

   ③ 检查_____修复文件。   ④ _____打印材料。

2. 看词语练拼音。Look at the words and practice Pinyin.

| kòngzhì | jìnxíng | bìng | bùzhòu |
| 控制 | 进行 | 并 | 步骤 |

| chéng | kāiqǐ | shèbèi | qián |
| 成 | 开启 | 设备 | 前 |

3. 朗读下列句子。Read aloud the following sentences.

1 Bǎ wénjiàn dǎorù kòngzhì diànnǎo qián, xūyào jìnxíng yùchǔlǐ ma?
把 文件 导入 控制 电脑 前，需要 进行 预处理 吗？

2 Duì móxíng jìnxíng qiēpiàn bìng tiānjiā zhīchēng.
对 模型 进行 切片 并 添加 支撑。

第6课 Lesson 6

模型后处理 Móxíng hòuchǔlǐ
Model Postprocessing

 复习 Revision

1. 根据图片选择词语。 Choose the words based on the pictures.

❶ 电脑（　　）　　❷ 技术（　　）　　❸ 转换（　　）
　 产品（　　）　　　 步骤（　　）　　　 变形（　　）

2. 把下列词语组合成短语或句子。 Connect the words into phrases or sentences.

❶　①文件　　②电脑　　③把　　④导入

_____

❷　①检查　　②文件　　③并　　④修复

_____

51

3 ①模型　②切片　③进行　④对

_____

热身 Warm-up

你认识这些词语吗？ Do you know these words?

 — qīnglǐ 清理 — clean

 — pāoguāng 抛光 — polish

 — jīnshǔ 金属 — metal

 — fěnmò 粉末 — powder

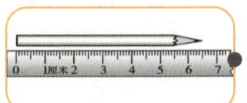 — cèliáng 测量 — measure

 — rèchǔlǐ 热处理 — heat treatment

第6课 | 模型后处理

 学习生词 Words and Expressions 06-01

1	后处理	hòuchǔlǐ	v.	postprocess
2	非金属	fēijīnshǔ	n.	non-metal
3	表面	biǎomiàn	n.	surface
4	清理	qīnglǐ	v.	clean, clean up
5	去除	qùchú	v.	remove
6	固化	gùhuà	v.	solidify, cure
7	打磨	dǎmó	v.	grind, sand
8	抛光	pāoguāng	v.	polish
9	喷绘	pēnhuì	v.	spray painting, spray printing
10	金属	jīnshǔ	n.	metal
11	粉末	fěnmò	n.	powder
12	测量	cèliáng	v.	measure
13	尺寸	chǐcùn	n.	dimension
14	以及	yǐjí	conj.	and
15	热处理	rèchǔlǐ	v.	heat treatment

词语练习 Word Exercises

1. 学习词语搭配。 Study the collocations.

❶ qīnglǐ 清理	qīnglǐ fěnmò 清理 粉末	clean the powder
	qīnglǐ diànnǎo 清理 电脑	clean up the computer
❷ dǎmó 打磨	dǎmó biǎomiàn 打磨 表面	sand the surface
	dǎmó shèbèi 打磨 设备	sand the equipment
❸ jīnshǔ 金属	jīnshǔ chéngxíng 金属 成型	metal forming
	jīnshǔ chǎnpǐn 金属 产品	metal products

2. 给词语选择正确搭配。 Choose the right words to form collocations.

❶ qùchú
去除_____
　　　　　　zhīchēng　　　　　chǐcùn
　　　　　A. 支撑　　　　B. 尺寸

❷ pāoguāng
抛光_____
　　　　　　biǎomiàn　　　　　cuòwù
　　　　　A. 表面　　　　B. 错误

❸ cèliáng
测量_____
　　　　　　chǐcùn　　　　　　géshi
　　　　　A. 尺寸　　　　B. 格式

第6课 | 模型后处理

 **学习课文** Text 🎧 06-02

非金属 零件 打印 完成 后，需要 进行 表面 清理、去除 支撑、固化、打磨、抛光、喷绘 等 处理。

金属 零件 打印 完成 后，需要 进行 粉末 清理、去除 支撑、测量 尺寸 等 处理，还 需要 进行 打磨 以及 热处理。

After non-metal parts are printed, surface cleaning, support removal, curing, sanding, polishing, and spray painting are required.

After metal parts are printed, powder cleaning, support removal, dimensional measurement, as well as sanding and heat treatment are necessary.

课文练习 Text Exercises

1. 回答问题。Answer the questions.

   ① 零件打印完成后需要去除支撑吗?

   ② 金属零件可以进行热处理吗?

2. 根据课文选词填空。Choose the words to fill in the blanks based on the text.

   | A. 热处理 | B. 清理 | C. 打磨 | D. 完成 |

   ① 非金属零件打印完成后可进行_____、抛光。

   ② 金属零件打印_____后,清理表面粉末。

学习语法 Grammar

 语法点 1 Grammar Point 1

助词"等" The particle "等"

It indicates unexhausted enumeration and it can also be expressed as "等等".

① 需要进行打磨、抛光、喷绘等处理。

② 增材制造技术可以制造工业产品、机械零件等。

③ 需要设定层厚、壁厚等参数。

选词填空。Choose the words to fill in the blanks.

> A. 等　　　B. 和

1. 增材制造技术可以制造工业产品、机械零件_____。
2. 需要设定层厚_____壁厚。
3. 我们需要进行打磨、抛光、喷绘_____处理。
4. 老师_____同学们对我很好。

语法点 2　Grammar Point 2

> **副词"还"　The adverb "还"**
>
> It is used before a verb to indicate that there is a supplement beyond a certain scope.
>
> 1. 零件打印完成后,需要进行表面清理、去除支撑,还需要进行打磨。
> 2. 打印文件的时候,需要转换文件格式,还需要准备打印材料。
> 3. 增材制造打印前需要建模,还需要进行预处理。

给"还"选择正确的位置。Choose the right positions for "还".

1. A 表面清理后 B,C 需要去除支撑。　　　　　　　　　(　　)
2. 我 A 会打开 B 文件,C 会创建文件。　　　　　　　　(　　)
3. 3D 打印 A 可以 B 制造工业产品,C 可以做什么?　　(　　)
4. A 设定层厚和壁厚后 B,C 需要设定什么参数?　　　(　　)

 汉字书写 Writing Chinese Characters

 职业拓展 Career Insight

Not all suspension models require the addition of supporting structures. If the angle of inclination between the suspended object and the vertical direction is less than 45°, adding support is not necessary. But if the angle exceeds 45°, support must 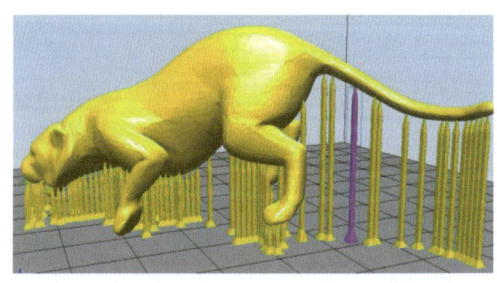 be added. As a result, it is essential to understand the suspension capabilities of your printer before initiating the printing process.

第 6 课 | 模型后处理

 小结 Summary

1. 听句子选词填空。Listen to the sentences and choose the words to fill in the blanks. 06-03

| A. 去除 | B. 热处理 | C. 清理 | D. 表面 |

❶ 非金属零件打印完成后，需要进行_____清理。

❷ 非金属零件打印完成后，需要_____支撑、抛光等处理。

❸ 金属零件打印完成后，需要进行粉末_____。

❹ 金属零件打印完成后，还需要进行打磨以及_____。

2. 看词语练拼音。Look at the words and practice Pinyin.

qīnglǐ 清理　　dǎmó 打磨　　pēnhuì 喷绘　　gùhuà 固化

fěnmò 粉末　　yǐjí 以及　　cèliáng 测量　　chǐcùn 尺寸

3. 朗读下列句子。Read aloud the following sentences.

❶ Fēijīnshǔ língjiàn dǎyìn wánchéng hòu, xūyào jìnxíng biǎomiàn qīnglǐ.
非金属 零件 打印 完成 后，需要 进行 表面 清理。

❷ Jīnshǔ língjiàn dǎyìn wánchéng hòu, hái xūyào jìnxíng dǎmó yǐjí rèchǔlǐ.
金属 零件 打印 完成 后，还 需要 进行 打磨 以及 热处理。

第7课 Lesson 7

三维扫描 Sānwéi sǎomiáo
3D Scanning

 复习 Revision

1. 根据图片选择词语。Choose the words based on the pictures.

❶ 金属（　　）　　❷ 打印（　　）　　❸ 物体（　　）
　 图形（　　）　　　 抛光（　　）　　　 粉末（　　）

2. 把下列词语组合成短语或句子。Connect the words into phrases or sentences.

1 ①零件　②后　③完成　④打印

_____

2 ①需要　②清理　③进行　④表面

_____

第7课 | 三维扫描

3 ①去除　②需要　③支撑　④零件

_____

 **热身 Warm-up**

你认识这些词语吗？ Do you know these words?

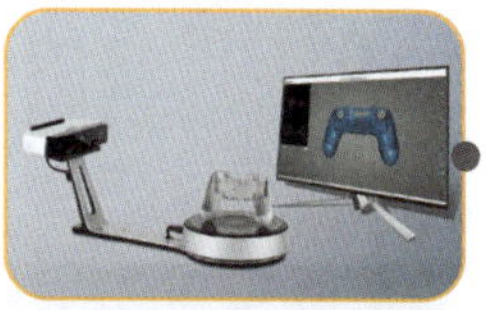

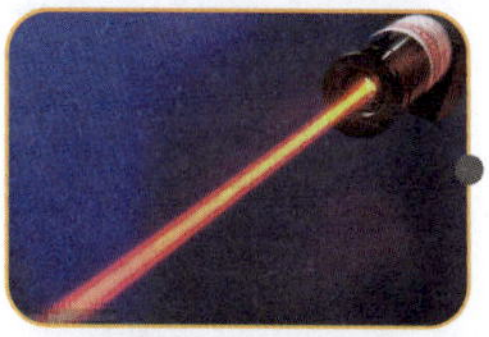

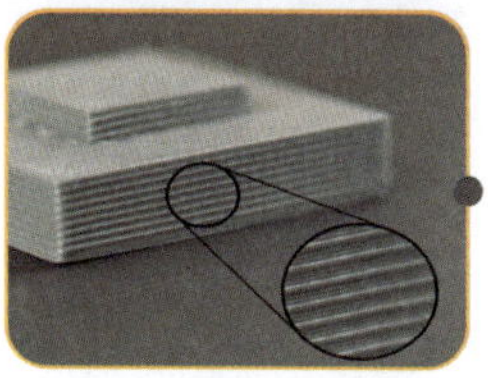

	sǎomiáo 扫描	scan
	jīguāng 激光	laser
	mìjí 密集	dense
	xìnxī 信息	information
	wénlǐ 纹理	texture
	yǐngxiàng 影像	image

61

学习生词 Words and Expressions 🎧 07-01

1	扫描	sǎomiáo	*v.*	scan
2	通过	tōngguò	*prep.*	through
3	激光	jīguāng	*n.*	laser
4	测距	cèjù	*v.*	measure a distance, find the range (of)
5	原理	yuánlǐ	*n.*	principle, theory
6	获取	huòqǔ	*v.*	acquire, obtain
7	物体	wùtǐ	*n.*	object
8	大量	dàliàng	*adj.*	a large amount of
9	密集	mìjí	*adj.*	dense
10	数据	shùjù	*n.*	data
11	信息	xìnxī	*n.*	information
12	坐标	zuòbiāo	*n.*	coordinate
13	纹理	wénlǐ	*n.*	texture
14	形成	xíngchéng	*v.*	form
15	建立	jiànlì	*v.*	establish
16	影像	yǐngxiàng	*n.*	image

第 7 课 | 三维扫描

词语练习 Word Exercises

1. 学习词语搭配。Study the collocations.

① sǎomiáo 扫描	sǎomiáo wùtǐ 扫描 物体	scan an object
	sǎomiáo móxíng 扫描 模型	scan a model
② huòqǔ 获取	huòqǔ shùjù 获取 数据	acquire data
	huòqǔ xìnxī 获取 信息	acquire information
③ jiànlì 建立	jiànlì móxíng 建立 模型	establish a model
	jiànlì wénjiàn 建立 文件	create a file

2. 给词语选择正确搭配。Choose the right words to form collocations.

① dàliàng 大量 _____　　A. shùjù 数据　　B. jīguāng 激光

② cèjù 测距 _____　　A. yuánlǐ 原理　　B. chǐcùn 尺寸

③ sānwéi 三维 _____　　A. zuòbiāo 坐标　　B. wénlǐ 纹理

学习课文 Text 🎧 07-02

三维激光扫描技术可以通过激光测距原理，获取物体表面大量密集的数据信息，例如三维坐标、表面纹理等，快速建立模型并形成图形数据，是快速建立物体三维影像模型的技术。

The 3D laser scanning technology, based on the principle of laser ranging, obtains a large amount of dense data from the surface of objects. For example, it can obtain 3D coordinates and surface textures, and quickly establish models and graphic data. It is a technology for rapidly creating three-dimensional image models of objects.

课文练习 Text Exercises

1. 回答问题。Answer the questions.

    ① 三维激光扫描技术的原理是激光测距吗？

    ② 通过激光扫描可获取物体表面大量密集的数据信息吗？

2. 根据课文选词填空。Choose the words to fill in the blanks based on the text.

    > A. 数据　　　B. 物体　　　C. 纹理　　　D. 原理

    ① 通过激光扫描获取物体表面_____信息。

    ② 可以快速建立模型并形成图形_____。

学习语法 Grammar

 语法点 1　Grammar Point 1

介词"通过"　The preposition "通过"

　　It is used to introduce the medium or means of an action. The common structure is: 通过…… + verbal phrase.

① 可以通过获取物体表面数据信息，快速建立三维模型。

② 可以通过添加支撑，防止模型变形。

③ 可以通过激光测距原理，获取物体表面数据信息。

选词填空。Choose the words to fill in the blanks.

> A. 对　　　　B. 通过

1. _____模型进行预处理。
2. _____添加支撑，可以防止模型变形。
3. _____文件格式进行转换。
4. _____获取物体表面大量数据信息，可以快速建立三维模型。

语法点 2　Grammar Point 2

> **动词"例如"　The verb "例如"**
>
> It is used to provide examples.
>
> 1. 我们可以获取物体表面数据信息，例如三维坐标和纹理。
> 2. 增材制造技术可以制造物体，例如工业产品和机械零件。
> 3. 切片的时候，需要设定参数，例如层厚和壁厚。

选词填空。Choose the words to fill in the blanks.

> A. 例如　　　　B. 等

1. 增材制造技术可以制造工业产品、机械零件_____。
2. 增材制造技术可以制造物体，_____工业产品和机械零件。
3. 需要进行打磨、抛光、喷绘_____处理。
4. 切片的时候，需要设定参数，_____层厚和壁厚。

第 7 课 | 三维扫描

 汉字书写 Writing Chinese Characters

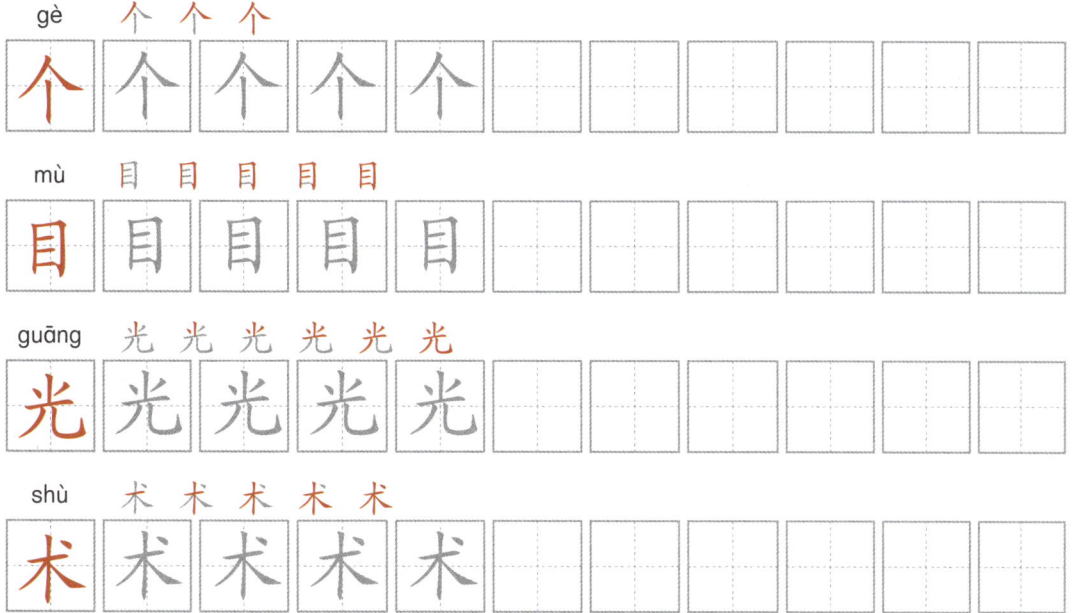

 文化拓展 Culture Insight

Beijing Opera, recognized as one of China's national treasures, stands as the most influential form of traditional Chinese opera. Originating in Beijing, it has gained widespread popularity across the country. Renowned for its portrayal of historical narratives, Beijing Opera boasts a repertoire of over 1,000 traditional plays. In 2006, it was included in the first batch of national intangible cultural heritages, endorsed by the State Council. In 2010, it was inscribed on UNESCO's Representative List of the Intangible Cultural Heritage of Humanity.

小结 Summary

1. 听句子选词填空。Listen to the sentences and choose the words to fill in the blanks. 07-03

> A. 密集　　　　B. 建立　　　　C. 通过　　　　D. 影像

1. 三维激光扫描技术_____激光测距原理获取数据信息。
2. 获取物体表面大量_____的数据信息。
3. 可以快速_____模型并形成图形数据。
4. 三维激光扫描技术是快速建立物体三维_____模型的技术。

2. 看词语练拼音。Look at the words and practice Pinyin.

huòqǔ	dàliàng	shùjù	yǐngxiàng
获取	大量	数据	影像
cèjù	jīguāng	mìjí	sǎomiáo
测距	激光	密集	扫描

3. 朗读下列句子。Read aloud the following sentences.

1. Sānwéi jīguāng sǎomiáo jìshù tōngguò jīguāng cèjù yuánlǐ huòqǔ shùjù xìnxī.
   三维 激光 扫描 技术 通过 激光 测距 原理 获取 数据 信息。

2. Lìrú sānwéi zuòbiāo、biǎomiàn wénlǐ děng.
   例如 三维 坐标、表面 纹理 等。

第8课 Lesson 8

逆向设计 Nìxiàng shèjì
Reverse Design

 复习 Revision

1. 根据图片选择词语。Choose the words based on the pictures.

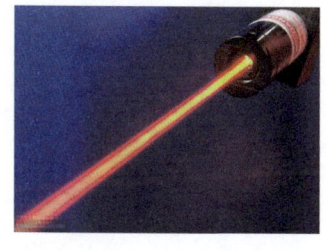  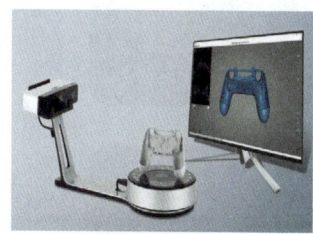

① 激光（　　）　　② 数据（　　）　　③ 扫描（　　）
　 物体（　　）　　　 影像（　　）　　　 获取（　　）

2. 把下列词语组合成短语或句子。Connect the words into phrases or sentences.

❶ ①扫描　　②通过　　③激光　　④物体

_____

❷ ①信息　　②获取　　③建立　　④模型

_____

3 ①技术　　②激光　　③三维　　④扫描

 热身 Warm-up

你认识这些词语吗？ Do you know these words?

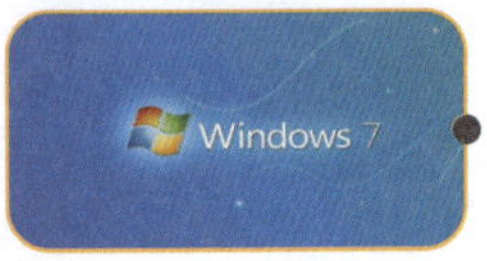

	nìxiàng 逆向	reverse
	shùzìhuà 数字化	digitize
	cǎijí 采集	collect
	gòuzào 构造	construct
	fēnxī 分析	analysis
	xìtǒng 系统	system

第 8 课 | 逆向设计

 学习生词 **Words and Expressions** 08-01

1	逆向	nìxiàng	*v.*	reverse
2	设计	shèjì	*v.*	design
3	对	duì	*prep.*	for
4	数字化	shùzìhuà	*v.*	digitize
5	采集	cǎijí	*v.*	collect
6	利用	lìyòng	*v.*	utilize, use
7	实现	shíxiàn	*v.*	achieve, realize
8	重新	chóngxīn	*adv.*	re-, again
9	构造	gòuzào	*v.*	construct
10	使用	shǐyòng	*v.*	use, employ
11	系统	xìtǒng	*n.*	system
12	分析	fēnxī	*v.*	analyze
13	再	zài	*adv.*	re-, again
14	编辑	biānjí	*v.*	edit

词语练习 Word Exercises

1. 学习词语搭配。Study the collocations.

❶ cǎijí 采集	cǎijí shùjù 采集 数据	collect data
	cǎijí xìnxī 采集 信息	collect information
❷ shǐyòng 使用	shǐyòng shèbèi 使用 设备	use equipment
	shǐyòng jīqì 使用 机器	use machines
❸ fēnxī 分析	fēnxī shùjù 分析 数据	analyze data
	fēnxī zhìliàng 分析 质量	analyze quality

2. 给词语选择正确搭配。Choose the right words to form collocations.

❶ gòuzào 构造 _____ A. jīqì 机器 B. móxíng 模型

❷ nìxiàng 逆向 _____ A. shèjì 设计 B. cáiliào 材料

❸ ruǎnjiàn 软件 _____ A. jīngdù 精度 B. xìtǒng 系统

第8课 | 逆向设计

 学习课文 Text 🎧 08-02

Nìxiàng shèjì kěyǐ duì chǎnpǐn biǎomiàn jìnxíng shùzìhuà
逆向设计可以对产品表面进行数字化
chǔlǐ (shùjù cǎijí、 shùjù chǔlǐ), lìyòng kěyǐ shíxiàn
处理（数据采集、数据处理），利用可以实现
nìxiàng sānwéi móxíng shèjì de ruǎnjiàn, chóngxīn gòuzào wùtǐ
逆向三维模型设计的软件，重新构造物体
de sānwéi móxíng, bìng shǐyòng ruǎnjiàn xìtǒng shíxiàn fēnxī、 zài
的三维模型，并使用软件系统实现分析、再
shèjì、 móxíng biānjí.
设计、模型编辑。

Digitally process the product surface (data collection, data processing), utilize software capable of reverse 3D model design to reconstruct the 3D model of the object, and employ software systems to achieve analysis, redesign, and model editing.

课文练习 Text Exercises

1. 回答问题。Answer the questions.

① 逆向设计可对产品表面进行数字化处理吗？

② 逆向设计可重新构造物体的三维模型吗？

2. 根据课文选词填空。Choose the words to fill in the blanks based on the text.

> A. 设计　　　B. 实现　　　C. 构造　　　D. 使用

1 _____软件系统可实现模型的再设计和编辑。

2 重新_____物体的三维模型。

学习语法 Grammar

语法点1　Grammar Point 1

副词"重新"　The adverb "重新"

It is used before a verb to indicate repeating a previous action.

1 利用软件重新构造物体的三维模型。

2 请重新打开软件。

3 参数需要重新设定。

把下列词语组合成短语或句子。Connect the words into phrases or sentences.

1 重新　　利用　　模型　　软件　　构造

_____

2 可以　　打印　　重新　　吗

_____

3 请 参数 设定 重新

_____

4 打开 需要 软件 重新

_____

语法点 2 Grammar Point 2

副词"再" The adverb "再"

It is used before a verb to indicate "once again" or repeating an action.

1 使用软件系统实现分析、再设计。

2 参数不对,请再设定一遍。

3 请你再说一遍。

选词填空。Choose the words to fill in the blanks.

A. 再   B. 在

1 使用软件系统实现分析与_____设计。

2 _____生产中,3D 打印可以做什么?

3 请你_____读一遍。

4 增材制造技术可以用_____制造零件上吗?

汉字书写 Writing Chinese Characters

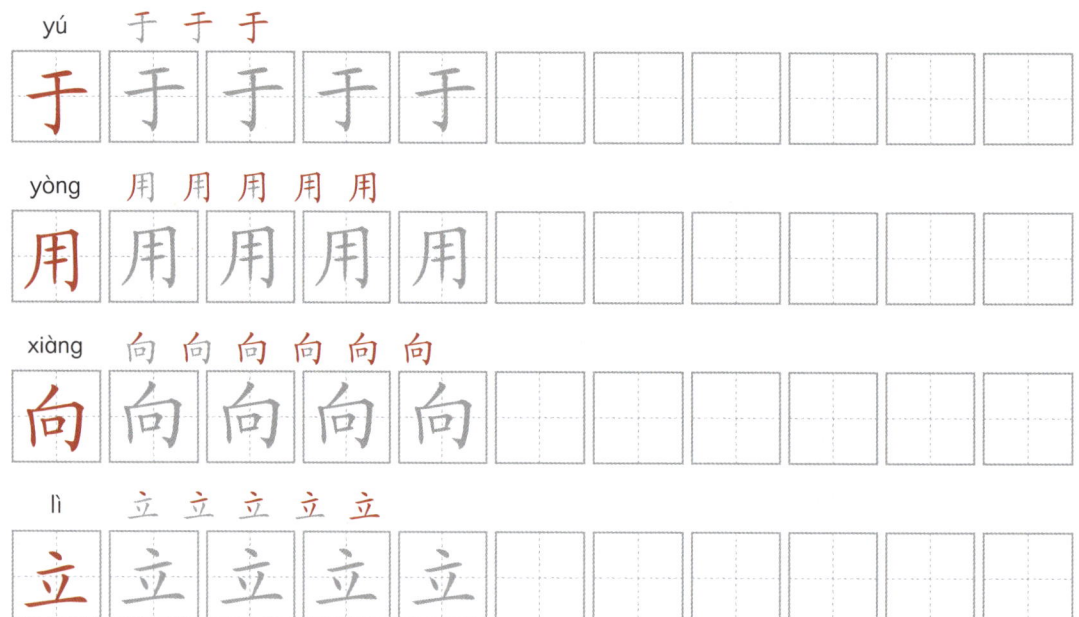

职业拓展 Career Insight

The forward design method reveals its limitations when applied to complex products, characterized by a high difficulty coefficient, prolonged cycles, elevated costs, and challenging research and development processes. Consequently, the reverse design method has naturally emerged and evolved as a solution.

第 8 课 | 逆向设计

 小结 Summary

1. 听句子选词填空。 Listen to the sentences and choose the words to fill in the blanks. 🎧 08-03

| A. 实现   B. 重新   C. 逆向   D. 对 |

❶ 逆向设计可以_____产品表面进行数字化处理。

❷ 利用可以实现_____三维模型设计的软件。

❸ _____构造物体的三维模型。

❹ 使用软件系统_____分析、再设计。

2. 看词语练拼音。 Look at the words and practice Pinyin.

shùzìhuà	chóngxīn	lìyòng	zài
数字化	重新	利用	再
xìtǒng	cǎijí	duì	shíxiàn
系统	采集	对	实现

3. 朗读下列句子。 Read aloud the following sentences.

❶ Nìxiàng shèjì kěyǐ duì chǎnpǐn biǎomiàn jìnxíng shùzìhuà chǔlǐ (shùjù cǎijí、 shùjù chǔlǐ).
逆向 设计 可以 对 产品 表面 进行 数字化 处理（数据 采集、数据 处理）。

❷ Chóngxīn gòuzào wùtǐ de sānwéi móxíng, bìng shǐyòng ruǎnjiàn xìtǒng shíxiàn fēnxī、 zài shèjì、 móxíng biānjí.
重新 构造 物体 的 三维 模型，并 使用 软件 系统 实现 分析、再 设计、模型 编辑。

77

第9课 Lesson 9

Róngróng chénjī chéngxíng
熔融沉积成型
Fused Deposition Modeling

 复习 Revision

1. 根据图片选择词语。Choose the words based on the pictures.

❶ 利用（　　）　　　❷ 设计（　　　）　　　❸ 系统（　　　）
　 构造（　　）　　　　 数字化（　　　）　　　　采集（　　　）

2. 把下列词语组合成短语或句子。Connect the words into phrases or sentences.

❶ ①进行　②数字化　③产品表面　④处理　⑤对

　　_____

❷ ①模型　②三维　③重新　④构造

　　_____

78

第 9 课 | 熔融沉积成型

3 ①使用　②分析　③实现　④软件系统

_____

热身 Warm-up

你认识这些词语吗？ Do you know these words?

	pēnzuǐ 喷嘴	nozzle
	jǐchū 挤出	extrude
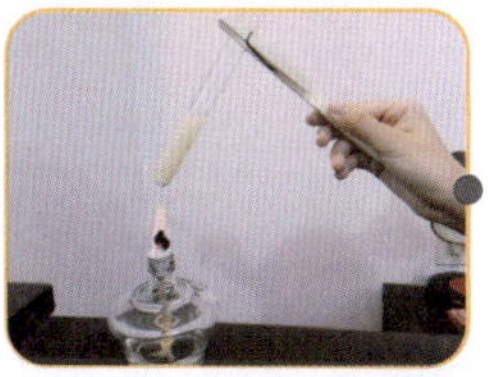	jiārè 加热	heat
	yètǐ 液体	liquid
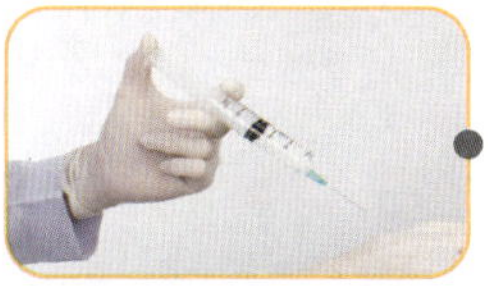	zhùrù 注入	inject
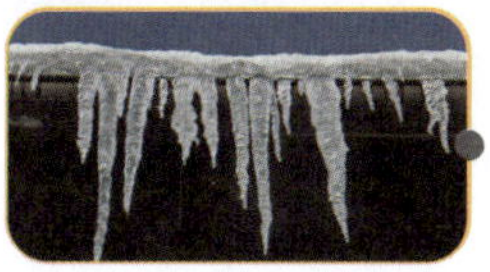	nínggù 凝固	solidify

79

学习生词 Words and Expressions 🎧 09-01

1	立体	lìtǐ	*adj.*	three-dimensional
2	拷贝	kǎobèi	*v.*	copy
3	到	dào	*v.*	used as a complement of a verb indicating the result of an action
4	装置	zhuāngzhì	*n.*	device
5	热塑性	rèsùxìng	*n.*	thermoplasticity
6	注入	zhùrù	*phr.*	inject
7	加热	jiā//rè	*v.*	heat
8	液体	yètǐ	*n.*	liquid
9	状态	zhuàngtài	*n.*	state
10	喷嘴	pēnzuǐ	*n.*	nozzle
11	沿着	yánzhe	*phr.*	along
12	移动	yídòng	*v.*	move
13	挤出	jǐchū	*phr.*	extrude
14	凝固	nínggù	*v.*	solidify
15	实物	shíwù	*n.*	physical object

第 9 课 | 熔融沉积成型

📖 词语练习 Word Exercises

1. 学习词语搭配。Study the collocations.

❶ jiārè 加热	jiārè yètǐ 加热 液体	heat the liquid
	jiārè zhuāngzhì 加热 装置	heating device
❷ yídòng 移动	yídòng wèizhì 移动 位置	change the position
	yídòng shèbèi 移动 设备	mobile equipment
❸ zhùrù 注入	zhùrù yètǐ 注入 液体	inject the liquid
	zhùrù cáiliào 注入 材料	inject the material

2. 给词语选择正确搭配。Choose the right words to form collocations.

❶ _____ móxíng 模型　　A. lìtǐ 立体　　B. zhōngxīn 中心

❷ _____ cáiliào 材料　　A. yánzhe 沿着　　B. jǐchū 挤出

❸ xíngchéng 形成_____　　A. jiārè 加热　　B. shíwù 实物

 学习课文　Text　🎧 09-02

第一步：利用软件建立立体模型。

第二步：将模型拷贝到控制装置。

第三步：将热塑性材料注入装置，并将材料加热到液体状态。

第四步：装置喷嘴沿着模型表面移动挤出材料。

第五步：材料凝固形成实物。

Step 1: Use software to establish a three-dimensional model.

Step 2: Copy the model to the control device.

Step 3: Inject thermoplastic material into the device and heat the material to a liquid state.

Step 4: The device nozzle moves along the surface of the model to extrude the material.

Step 5: The material solidifies to form a physical object.

第 9 课 ｜ 熔融沉积成型

课文练习 Text Exercises

1. 回答问题。Answer the questions.

① 要将热塑性材料注入装置并加热到液体状态吗？

② 挤出材料时，装置喷嘴会沿着模型表面移动吗？

2. 根据课文选词填空。Choose the words to fill in the blanks based on the text.

> A. 注入　　　B. 拷贝　　　C. 加热　　　D. 移动

① 将材料_____到液体状态。

② 装置喷嘴沿着模型表面_____挤出材料。

学习语法 Grammar

语法点 1　Grammar Point 1

介词"将"　The preposition "将"

The "将" sentence pattern has a meaning and function similar to those of the "把" sentence pattern, and "将" is often used in written Chinese.

① 将模型拷贝到控制装置。

② 将热塑性材料注入装置。

③ 将材料加热到液体状态。

连词成句。Connect the words into sentences.

1. 拷贝　将　模型　到　控制装置

_____

2. 请　分成　多层　将　模型

_____

3. 将　可以　用　哪儿　制造　技术　增材　在

_____

4. 加热　需要　状态　到　将　材料　液体

_____

语法点 2　Grammar Point 2

介词"沿"　The preposition "沿"

It is used to introduce the direction or path of an action or a behavior. The common structure is: 沿（着）(along) + noun + verbal phrase.

1. 沿着模型表面移动装置喷嘴。
2. 沿着哪儿移动装置喷嘴？
3. 请沿着零件表面进行打磨。

选词填空。Choose the words to fill in the blanks.

| A. 沿着　　　　B. 对 |

1. _____模型文件进行软件切片。
2. _____哪儿移动装置喷嘴？
3. 请_____零件表面进行打磨。
4. _____文件格式进行转换。

第 9 课 | 熔融沉积成型

 汉字书写 Writing Chinese Characters

 文化拓展 Culture Insight

Tea originated in China and was initially used as an offering in sacrifices. By the late Spring and Autumn period (770 B.C. – 476 B.C.), it began to be consumed as a vegetable, and by the mid-Western Han Dynasty (206 B.C. – 8 A.D.), it evolved into a form of medicine. Since the late Western Han Dynasty, tea has been regarded as a premium beverage for the royal court. The earliest evidence of artificial tea cultivation has been discovered at the Tianluo Mountain Site in Yuyao, Zhejiang, dating back over 6,000 years. Tea, typically oblong or elliptical in

85

shape, can be brewed in boiling water and is categorized into six types based on its variety, production method, and appearance.

 小结 Summary

1. 听句子选词填空。Listen to the sentences and choose the words to fill in the blanks. 🎧 09-03

> A. 拷贝　　　　B. 注入　　　　C. 凝固　　　　D. 立体

❶ 利用软件建立_____模型。

❷ 将模型_____到控制装置。

❸ 将热塑性材料_____装置。

❹ 材料_____形成实物。

2. 看词语练拼音。Look at the words and practice Pinyin.

| zhuāngzhì | rèsùxìng | zhùrù | jiārè |
| 装置 | 热塑性 | 注入 | 加热 |

| yètǐ | zhuàngtài | yánzhe | yídòng |
| 液体 | 状态 | 沿着 | 移动 |

3. 朗读下列句子。Read aloud the following sentences.

❶ Jiāng móxíng kǎobèi dào kòngzhì zhuāngzhì.
　将 模型 拷贝 到 控制 装置。

❷ Jiāng rèsùxìng cáiliào zhùrù zhuāngzhì, bìng jiāng cáiliào jiārè dào yètǐ zhuàngtài.
　将 热塑性 材料 注入 装置，并 将 材料 加热 到 液体 状态。

第10课 Lesson 10
Guānggùhuà chéngxíng
光固化成型
Stereolithography

 复习 Revision

1. 根据图片选择词语。Choose the words based on the pictures.

  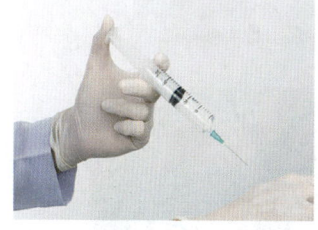

❶ 实物（   ）　　❷ 挤出（   ）　　❸ 拷贝（   ）
　 喷嘴（   ）　　　 液体（   ）　　　 注入（   ）

2. 把下列词语组合成短语或句子。Connect the words into phrases or sentences.

① ①形成　②实物　③材料　④凝固

_____

② ①软件　②利用　③模型　④建立

_____

3 ①到   ②加热   ③状态   ④液体

_____

热身 Warm-up

你认识这些词语吗？ Do you know these words?

 下降 xiàjiàng — lower

 连接 liánjiē — connect

 结束 jiéshù — end

 树脂 shùzhī — resin

 重复 chóngfù — repeat

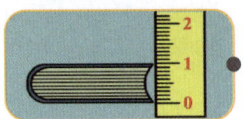 厚度 hòudù — thickness

第10课 光固化成型

 学习生词 Words and Expressions 🎧 10-01

1	光固化	guānggùhuà	phr.	photocuring
2	液槽	yècáo	n.	liquid tank
3	树脂	shùzhī	n.	resin
4	逐点	zhú diǎn	phr.	point by point
5	固化	gùhuà	v.	cure, solidify
6	每层	měi céng	phr.	each layer
7	二维	èrwéi	adj.	two-dimensional
8	结束	jiéshù	v.	end
9	升降台	shēngjiàngtái	n.	lifting platform
10	下降	xiàjiàng	v.	lower
11	高度	gāodù	n.	height
12	新	xīn	adj.	new
13	连接	liánjiē	v.	connect
14	重复	chóngfù	v.	repeat

词语练习 Word Exercises

1. 学习词语搭配。 Study the collocations.

	chóngfù bùzhòu 重复 步骤	repeat the steps
❶ chóngfù 重复	chóngfù lìyòng 重复 利用	reuse
❷ liánjiē 连接	liánjiē diànnǎo 连接 电脑	connect a computer
	liánjiē shèbèi 连接 设备	connecting devices
❸ xiàjiàng 下降	shēngjiàngtái xiàjiàng 升降台 下降	the lifting platform lowers
	wèizhì xiàjiàng 位置 下降	the position lowers

2. 给词语选择正确搭配。 Choose the right words to form collocations.

❶ zhùrù
注入_____   A. shùzhī 树脂   B. yècáo 液槽

❷ chóngfù
重复_____   A. èrwéi 二维   B. bùzhòu 步骤

❸ zhúdiǎn
逐点_____   A. sǎomiáo 扫描   B. gāodù 高度

第 10 课 | 光固化成型

 学习课文 Text 🎧 10-02

第一步:在液槽中注入光固化树脂。

第二步:利用激光逐点扫描固化树脂。

第三步:每层固化后,树脂形成二维图形。

第四步:结束后,升降台下降一层高度,进行下一层扫描。

第五步:将新固化的一层和前一层连接,重复上一个步骤,直到成型结束。

Step 1: Inject photocurable resin into the liquid tank.

Step 2: Use a laser to scan the curable resin point by point.

> Step 3: After each layer is cured, the resin forms a two-dimensional pattern.
>
> Step 4: After completion, the lifting platform lowers by one layer of height to perform the scan of the next layer.
>
> Step 5: Connect the newly-cured layer to the previous layer and repeat the previous step until the molding is complete.

课文练习 Text Exercises

1. 回答问题。Answer the questions.

① 每层固化后,树脂形成了几维图形?

② 固化完一层后升降台需要下降吗?

2. 根据课文选词填空。Choose the words to fill in the blanks based on the text.

A. 重复　　B. 高度　　C. 形成　　D. 固化

① _____ 上一个步骤,直到成型结束。

② 利用激光逐点扫描 _____ 树脂。

第10课 | 光固化成型

学习语法 Grammar

语法点 1　Grammar Point 1

动词性词语 + 后 / 以后 / 之后　Verbal phrase + 后 / 以后 / 之后

It is used as an adverbial modifier in a sentence to indicate "after a certain time".

1. 每层固化后，树脂形成二维图形。
2. 结束后，升降台下降一层高度。
3. 打印完成后，需要清理表面粉末。

选词填空。Choose the words to fill in the blanks.

A. 后　　　B. 并

1. 每层固化_____，树脂形成一个二维图形。
2. 对模型进行软件切片，_____添加支撑。
3. 结束_____，升降台下降一层高度。
4. 打开工作界面，_____选择"创建文件"。

语法点 2　Grammar Point 2

……，直到……　..., until...

It is used to indicate that an action or state continues until a certain point in time approaches or a certain situation occurs.

1. 重复上一个步骤，直到成型结束。
2. 沿着模型表面移动挤出材料，直到凝固形成实物。
3. 重复前一个步骤，直到模型打印完成。

选词填空。Choose the words to fill in the blanks.

A. 直到　　　　B. 通过

1. 重复上一个步骤，_____成型结束。
2. _____添加支撑，可以防止模型变形。
3. 沿着模型表面移动挤出材料，_____凝固形成实物。
4. 还可以_____快速成型，建立目标的三维模型。

 汉字书写　Writing Chinese Characters

tái
台　台　台　台　台　台

chéng
成　成　成　成　成　成

shù
束　束　束　束　束　束

mù
木　木　木　木　木

职业拓展 Career Insight

Photocurable resin, also referred to as photosensitive resin, is a type of oligomer that undergoes rapid physical and chemical transformations upon exposure to light, leading to crosslinking and curing. This resin, characterized by a relatively low molecular weight, contains reactive groups that facilitate the photocuring process.

小结 Summary

1. 听句子选词填空。Listen to the sentences and choose the words to fill in the blanks. 10-03

> A. 高度　　　B. 每层　　　C. 光固化　　　D. 逐点

❶ 在液槽中注入_____树脂。

❷ 利用激光_____扫描固化树脂。

❸ _____固化后，树脂形成二维图形。

❹ 一层固化结束后，升降台下降一层_____，进行下一层扫描。

2. 看词语练拼音。Look at the words and practice Pinyin.

| guānggùhuà | shùzhī | měi céng | xíngchéng |
| 光固化 | 树脂 | 每 层 | 形成 |

| èrwéi | jiéshù | xīn | chóngfù |
| 二维 | 结束 | 新 | 重复 |

3. 朗读下列句子。Read aloud the following sentences.

❶ Lìyòng jīguāng zhú diǎn sǎomiáo gùhuà shùzhī.
利用 激光 逐点 扫描 固化 树脂。

❷ Shēngjiàngtái xiàjiàng yì céng gāodù, jìnxíng xià yì céng sǎomiáo.
升降台 下降 一 层 高度，进行 下 一 层 扫描。

第11课 Lesson 11

激光成型 Jīguāng chéngxíng
Laser Forming

 复习 Revision

1. 根据图片选择词语。Choose the words based on the pictures.

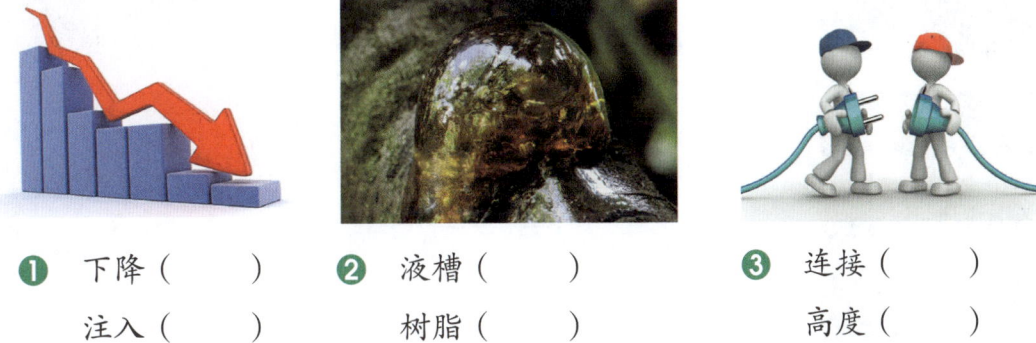

① 下降（　　）　　② 液槽（　　）　　③ 连接（　　）
　 注入（　　）　　　 树脂（　　）　　　 高度（　　）

2. 把下列词语组合成短语或句子。Connect the words into phrases or sentences.

① ①逐点　②扫描　③激光　④利用

_____

② ①后　②固化　③图形　④形成

_____

3 ①直到　②重复　③步骤　④结束

热身 Warm-up

你认识这些词语吗？ Do you know these words?

 (发光能量图)	néngliàng 能量	energy
 (铺平地面图)	pūpíng 铺平	level, flatten
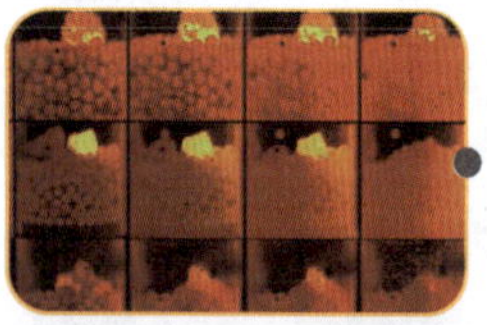 (粉末样品图)	shāojié 烧结	sinter
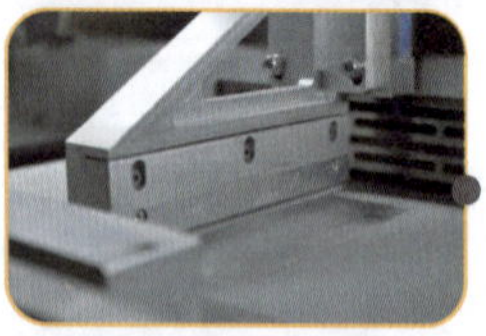 (铺粉设备图)	pūfěn 铺粉	spread powder
 (金属毛坯图)	máopī 毛坯	blank
 (播放按钮图)	kāishǐ 开始	start

学习生词 Words and Expressions 11-01

1	向	xiàng	*prep.*	to, towards
2	加入	jiārù	*v.*	add
3	固定	gùdìng	*adj.*	fixed, settled
4	能量	néngliàng	*n.*	energy
5	密度	mìdù	*n.*	density
6	逐层	zhú céng	*phr.*	layer by layer
7	烧结	shāojié	*v.*	sinter
8	有	yǒu	*prep.*	with
9	片层	piàncéng	*n.*	layer
10	基板	jībǎn	*n.*	substrate
11	铺粉	pūfěn	*v.*	spread powder
12	再次	zàicì	*adv.*	re-, again
13	铺平	pūpíng	*phr.*	level, flatten, smooth
14	开始	kāishǐ	*v.*	start
15	毛坯	máopī	*n.*	blank, rough casting

词语练习 Word Exercises

1. 学习词语搭配。Study the collocations.

❶ jiārù 加入	jiārù cáiliào 加入 材料	add materials
	jiārù fěnmò 加入 粉末	add powder
❷ kāishǐ 开始	kāishǐ dǎyìn 开始 打印	start printing
	kāishǐ sǎomiáo 开始 扫描	start scanning
❸ zàicì 再次	zàicì dǎkāi 再次 打开	open again
	zàicì pūpíng 再次 铺平	flatten again

2. 给词语选择正确搭配。Choose the right words to form collocations.

❶ néngliàng
能量_____   A. mìdù 密度   B. dǎmó 打磨

❷ pūfěn
铺粉_____   A. sǎomiáo 扫描   B. shèbèi 设备

❸ língjiàn
零件_____   A. máopī 毛坯   B. kāishǐ 开始

第11课 | 激光成型

 学习课文 Text 🎧 11-02

第一步：向设备加入金属粉末。

第二步：激光以固定的能量密度逐层进行扫描。

第三步：扫描后的粉末烧结成有厚度的片层。

第四步：基板下降，铺粉设备再次将粉末铺平。

第五步：开始新一层的扫描，重复打印步骤，可以制造零件毛坯。

Step 1: Add metal powder to the device.

Step 2: The laser scans layer by layer with a fixed energy density.

Step 3:　The scanned powder sinters into a thick layer.

Step 4:　The substrate descends, and the powder-spreading device levels the powder again.

Step 5:　Start scanning a new layer and repeat the printing steps to create a part blank.

课文练习　Text Exercises

1. 回答问题。Answer the questions.

❶ 重复打印步骤可以获得零件毛坯吗?

❷ 激光以不固定的能量密度逐层进行扫描,对吗?

2. 根据课文选词填空。Choose the words to fill in the blanks based on the text.

| A. 烧结 | B. 加入 | C. 毛坯 | D. 再次 |

❶ 向设备_____金属粉末。

❷ 扫描后的粉末_____成有厚度的片层。

第 11 课 | 激光成型

 学习语法 Grammar

语法点 1　Grammar Point 1

介词"向"　The preposition "向"

It is used to introduce the direction, target, or object of an action. The common structure is: 向 (to) + noun + verbal phrase.

1. 向设备加入金属粉末。
2. 向切片软件导入模型文件。
3. 向设备注入热塑性材料。

选词填空。Choose the words to fill in the blanks.

A. 在　　B. 向

1. 增材制造技术可以用_____工业产品制造上。
2. _____设备加入金属粉末。
3. _____工业中，3D 打印可以做什么？
4. _____装置注入热塑性材料。

语法点 2　Grammar Point 2

介词"以"　The preposition "以"

It is used to introduce the condition, method, means, tool, etc. associated with an action or a behavior. The common structure is: 以 + noun + verbal phrase.

103

1 激光以固定的能量密度逐层进行扫描。

2 这个文件以什么格式保存?

3 以相等的厚度进行分层切片。

选词填空。Choose the words to fill in the blanks.

A. 以　　B. 对

1 激光_____固定的能量密度逐层进行扫描。

2 _____模型进行软件切片。

3 _____文件格式进行转换。

4 这个文件_____什么格式保存?

汉字书写 Writing Chinese Characters

xiàng 向

piàn 片

yǐ 以

máo 毛

文化拓展 Culture Insight

Paper-making technology stands as one of the Four Great Inventions of ancient China. In the Eastern Han Dynasty (25 A.D.–220 A.D.), Cai Lun synthesized the experiences of his predecessors and refined the paper-making process by utilizing bark, hemp, rags, old fishing nets, and plant fibers as raw materials, having significantly improved the quality of paper. The fundamental paper-making technique he developed continues to be used to this day and has had a profound impact on the advancement of the global paper-making industry and the dissemination of human civilization.

小结 Summary

1. 听句子选词填空。Listen to the sentences and choose the words to fill in the blanks. 11-03

| A. 有 | B. 加入 | C. 开始 | D. 再次 |

❶ 铺粉设备_____将粉末铺平。

② _____ 新一层的扫描。

③ 向设备_____金属粉末。

④ 扫描后的粉末烧结成_____厚度的片层。

2. 看词语练拼音。Look at the words and practice Pinyin.

| gùdìng | néngliàng | zhú céng | piàncéng |
| 固定 | 能量 | 逐 层 | 片层 |

| jībǎn | pūfěn | pūpíng | kāishǐ |
| 基板 | 铺粉 | 铺平 | 开始 |

3. 朗读下列句子。Read aloud the following sentences.

① Jībǎn xiàjiàng, pūfěn shèbèi zàicì jiāng fěnmò pūpíng.
基板 下降，铺粉 设备 再次 将 粉末 铺平。

② Kāishǐ xīn yì céng de sǎomiáo, chóngfù dǎyìn bùzhòu, kěyǐ zhìzào língjiàn máopī.
开始 新 一 层 的 扫描，重复 打印 步骤，可以 制造 零件 毛坯。

第12课 3D打印机
Lesson 12 3D Printer

 复习 Revision

1. 根据图片选择词语。Choose the words based on the pictures.

 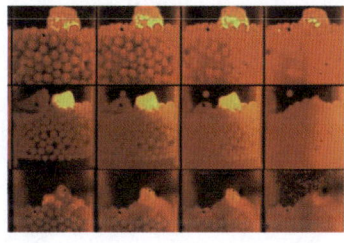 

❶ 能量（   ）　　❷ 开始（   ）　　❸ 毛坯（   ）
　 加入（   ）　　　 烧结（   ）　　　 密度（   ）

2. 把下列词语组合成短语或句子。Connect the words into phrases or sentences.

❶ ①设备　②加入　③向　④粉末

_____

❷ ①设备　②粉末　③将　④铺平

_____

107

3 ①制造　②毛坯　③零件　④可以

_____

热身 Warm-up

你认识这些词语吗？ Do you know these words?

 (3D printer image)	dǎyìnjī 打印机	printer
 (glue image)	niánhé 黏合	bond
 (plastic filament image)	sùliào 塑料	plastic
 (program icons image)	chéngxù 程序	program
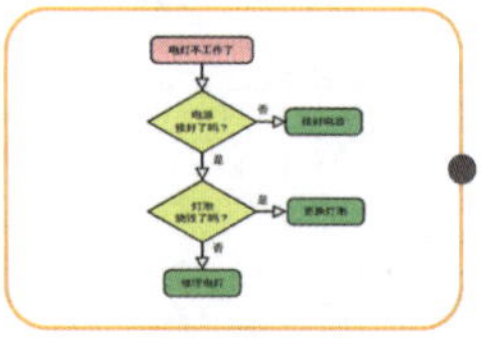 (flowchart image)	liúchéng 流程	process
 (brain/lightbulb image)	chuàngzào 创造	create

第 12 课 | 3D打印机

 学习生词 Words and Expressions 12-01

1	打印机	dǎyìnjī	*n.*	printer
2	即	jí	*v.*	i.e.
3	它	tā	*pron.*	it
4	基础	jīchǔ	*n.*	basis
5	运用	yùnyòng	*v.*	use, utilize
6	塑料	sùliào	*n.*	plastic
7	等	děng	*part.*	etc.
8	黏合	niánhé	*v.*	bond
9	或	huò	*conj.*	or
10	创造	chuàngzào	*v.*	create
11	流程	liúchéng	*n.*	process
12	分别	fēnbié	*adv.*	respectively
13	按照	ànzhào	*prep.*	according to
14	编制	biānzhì	*v.*	compile
15	程序	chéngxù	*n.*	program

词语练习 Word Exercises

1. 学习词语搭配。Study the collocations.

❶ yùnyòng 运用	yùnyòng jìshù 运用 技术	use technology
	yùnyòng xìnxī 运用 信息	use information
❷ liúchéng 流程	zhìzào liúchéng 制造 流程	manufacturing process
	dǎyìn liúchéng 打印 流程	printing process
❸ chéngxù 程序	biānzhì chéngxù 编制 程序	compile a program
	chéngxù shèjì 程序 设计	programming

2. 给词语选择正确搭配。Choose the right words to form collocations.

❶ niánhé
黏合_____　　A. cáiliào 材料　　B. shāojié 烧结

❷ _____chéngxù 程序　　A. sùliào 塑料　　B. biānzhì 编制

❸ _____sānwéi wùtǐ 三维 物体　　A. chuàngzào 创造　　B. fēnbié 分别

第 12 课 | 3D打印机

 **学习课文 Text** 🎧 12-02

3D打印机即三维打印机,它以数字模型为基础,运用塑料、树脂、金属等可黏合或可烧结的材料,通过逐层成型创造三维物体。制造流程是把数据和材料分别导入机器,机器按照编制的程序把产品一层层打印、创造出来。

A 3D printer, also known as a three-dimensional printer, creates three-dimensional objects based on digital models. Using materials such as plastics, resins, and metals that are bondable or sinterable it creates 3D objects through layer-by-layer formation. The manufacturing process begins with importing data and materials into the machine. The machine then prints and creates the product layer by layer according to the compiled program.

📖 **课文练习 Text Exercises**

1. 回答问题。Answer the questions.

① 3D 打印机和三维打印机一样吗？

② 塑料和树脂是可黏合、可烧结的材料吗？

2. 根据课文选词填空。Choose the words to fill in the blanks based on the text.

> A. 创造　　B. 黏合　　C. 程序　　D. 基础

① 以数字模型为_____。

② 运用树脂、金属等可_____或可烧结的材料。

 **学习语法 Grammar**

 语法点 1　Grammar Point 1

动词"即"　The verb "即"

It is used in written Chinese for emphasis or further explanation.

① 3D 打印机即三维打印机。

② 层厚即切片厚度。

③ 壁厚即模型外壳厚度。

选词填空。Choose the words to fill in the blanks.

A. 即 　　　 B. 和

1. 3D 打印机_____三维打印机。
2. 壁厚_____模型外壳厚度。
3. 需要设定层厚_____壁厚。
4. 我会操作第一步_____第二步。

语法点 2　Grammar Point 2

介词"按照"　The preposition "按照"

It is used to introduce the basis of an action or a behavior. The common structure is: 按照 + noun + verbal phrase.

1. 机器按照程序把产品一层层制造出来。
2. 按照什么步骤进行光固化成型？
3. 请按照下面五个步骤操作。

选词填空。Choose the words to fill in the blanks.

A. 按照 　　　 B. 沿着

1. 机器_____程序把产品一层层制造出来。
2. _____模型表面移动装置喷嘴。
3. _____什么步骤进行光固化成型？
4. 请_____零件表面进行打磨。

 汉字书写 Writing Chinese Characters

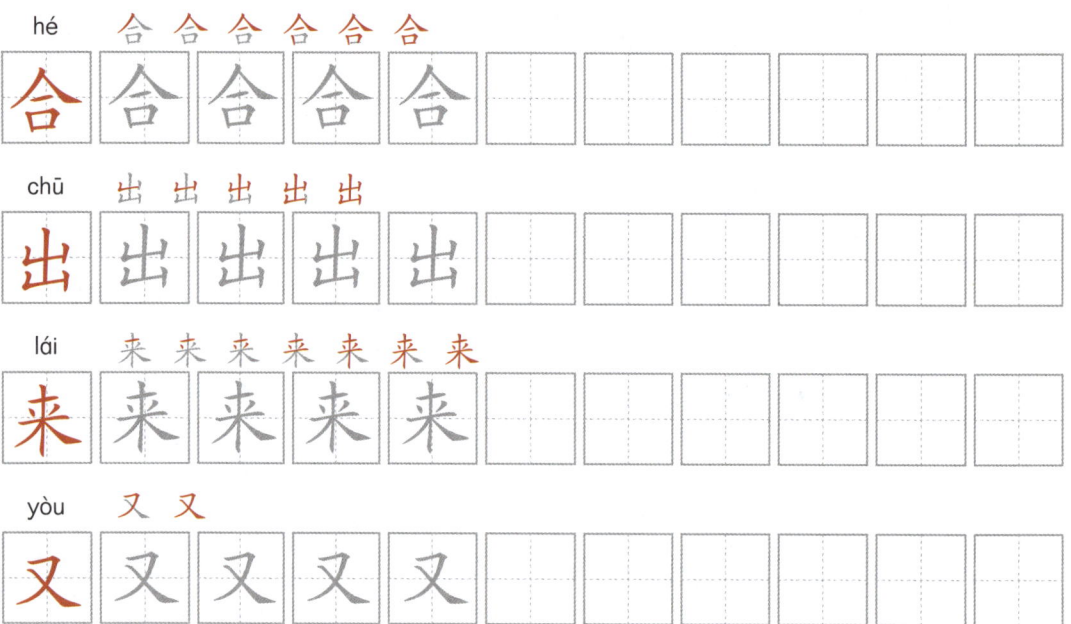

 职业拓展 Career Insight

The 3D printer emerged in the mid-1980s as a rapid prototyping device, operating on the same fundamental principles as conventional printing. Utilizing digital model files, it employs adhesive materials such as powdered metal or plastic to fabricate objects through a layer-by-layer printing process.

第 12 课 | 3D打印机

 小结 Summary

1. 听句子选词填空。Listen to the sentences and choose the words to fill in the blanks. 🎧 12-03

| A. 创造 | B. 分别 | C. 程序 | D. 基础 |

1. 3D 打印机即三维打印机，它以数字模型为_____。

2. 把数据和材料_____导入机器。

3. 通过逐层成型_____三维物体。

4. 机器按照编制的_____把产品一层层打印、创造出来。

2. 看词语练拼音。Look at the words and practice Pinyin.

dǎyìnjī	jīchǔ	yùnyòng	liúchéng
打印机	基础	运用	流程
fēnbié	ànzhào	biānzhì	chuàngzào
分别	按照	编制	创造

3. 朗读下列句子。Read aloud the following sentences.

1. Yùnyòng sùliào、shùzhī、jīnshǔ děng kěniánhé huò kěshāojié de cáiliào.
   运用 塑料、树脂、金属 等 可黏合 或 可烧结 的 材料。

2. Jīqì ànzhào biānzhì de chéngxù bǎ chǎnpǐn yì céngcéng dǎyìn、chuàngzào chulai.
   机器 按照 编制 的 程序 把 产品 一 层层 打印、创造 出来。

115

第13课 打印材料
Lesson 13 Printing Materials
Dǎyìn cáiliào

 复习 Revision

1. 根据图片选择词语。Choose the words based on the pictures.

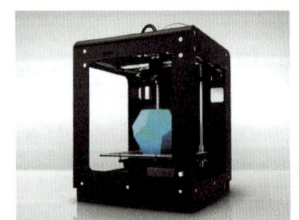  

❶ 打印机（　　）　　❷ 塑料（　　）　　❸ 黏合（　　）
　 流程（　　）　　　　树脂（　　）　　　 创造（　　）

2. 把下列词语组合成短语或句子。Connect the words into phrases or sentences.

[1] ①为基础　　②以　　③模型　　④数字

_____

[2] ①程序　　②产品　　③创造　　④按照

_____

第13课 | 打印材料

3 ①逐层　②创造　③物体　④成型

_____

热身 Warm-up

你认识这些词语吗？ Do you know these words?

shígāo 石膏	gypsum
táocí 陶瓷	ceramic
yánfā 研发	research and develop
gǔfěn 骨粉	bone powder
sīzhuàng 丝状	filamentous
gōngyì 工艺	process, technique

117

 学习生词 Words and Expressions 13-01

1	光敏	guāngmǐn	*adj.*	photosensitive
2	石膏	shígāo	*n.*	gypsum
3	陶瓷	táocí	*n.*	ceramic
4	生物	shēngwù	*n.*	biology
5	领域	lǐngyù	*n.*	field
6	人造	rénzào	*adj.*	artificial
7	骨粉	gǔfěn	*n.*	bone powder
8	原料	yuánliào	*n.*	raw material
9	这些	zhèxiē	*pron.*	these
10	针对	zhēnduì	*v.*	target at
11	工艺	gōngyì	*n.*	process, technique
12	研发	yánfā	*v.*	research and develop
13	不同	bù tóng	*phr.*	different
14	形态	xíngtài	*n.*	form
15	丝状	sīzhuàng	*n.*	filamentous

第 13 课｜打印材料

词语练习 Word Exercises

1. 学习词语搭配。Study the collocations.

❶ shēngwù 生物	shēngwù yuánliào 生物 原料	biological raw materials
	shēngwù cáiliào 生物 材料	biological materials
❷ zhèxiē 这些	zhèxiē cáiliào 这些 材料	these materials
	zhèxiē wénjiàn 这些 文件	these files
❸ gōngyì 工艺	zhìzào gōngyì 制造 工艺	manufacturing process
	gōngyì yánfā 工艺 研发	process research and development

2. 给词语选择正确搭配。Choose the right words to form collocations.

❶ shēngwù
　生物＿＿＿＿　　A. yuánliào 原料　　B. zhēnduì 针对

❷ ＿＿＿＿gǔfěn 骨粉　　A. rénzào 人造　　B. lǐngyù 领域

❸ bù tóng
　不 同＿＿＿＿　　A. xiāngděng 相等　　B. xíngtài 形态

119

学习课文 Text 🎧 13-02

3D dǎyìn shǐyòng de cáiliào yǒu sùliào、guāngmǐn shùzhī、
3D 打印使用的材料有塑料、光敏 树脂、
shígāo、jīnshǔ hé táocí děng, shēngwù lǐngyù shǐyòng de cáiliào yǒu
石膏、金属和陶瓷等，生物 领域 使用的材料有
rénzào gǔfěn、shēngwù yuánliào děng。 Zhèxiē cáiliào shì zhēnduì 3D
人造 骨粉、生物 原料 等。这些材料是针对 3D
dǎyìn shèbèi hé gōngyì yánfā de, yǒu bù tóng de xíngtài, lìrú
打印设备和 工艺研发的，有不同的形态，例如
fěnmò、sīzhuàng、yètǐ děng。
粉末、丝状、液体 等。

The materials used in 3D printing include plastics, photosensitive resins, gypsum, metals, and ceramics. In the biological field, materials such as artificial bone powder and biological raw materials are utilized. These materials are specifically developed for 3D printing equipment and processes, and come in various forms, such as powder, filaments, liquid, etc.

课文练习 Text Exercises

1. 回答问题。Answer the questions.

① 光敏树脂是 3D 打印中所使用的材料吗？

❷ 3D 打印中所使用的材料的形态包括粉末吗？

2. 根据课文选词填空。Choose the words to fill in the blanks based on the text.

> A. 研发　　　B. 工艺　　　C. 原料　　　D. 丝状

❶ 生物领域使用的材料有人造骨粉、生物_____等。

❷ 这些材料是针对 3D 打印设备和_____研发的。

学习语法 Grammar

语法点 1　Grammar Point 1

> **表领有的"有"字句**　"有" sentences indicating possession
>
> It is used to indicate that a whole object contains several parts, which are subordinate to the whole. The structure is: whole + 有 + part 1, part 2... part N.
>
> ❶ 3D 打印使用的材料有塑料、光敏树脂、石膏、金属和陶瓷等。
> ❷ 生物领域使用的材料有人造骨粉、生物原料等。
> ❸ 需要设定的参数有层厚和壁厚。

选词填空。Choose the words to fill in the blanks.

> A. 有　　　　　B. 例如

❶ 3D打印使用的材料_____塑料、光敏树脂、石膏、金属和陶瓷等。

❷ 3D打印使用的材料很多，_____塑料、光敏树脂、石膏、金属和陶瓷等。

❸ 操作切片软件的时候，需要设定很多参数，_____层厚和壁厚。

❹ 操作切片软件的时候，需要设定的参数_____层厚和壁厚。

语法点 2　Grammar Point 2

"是……的"句　"是……的" sentences

It is used to emphasize the time, location, method, etc. of an event that has occurred.

❶ 这些材料是针对3D打印设备和工艺研发的。

❷ 这个文件是以STL格式保存的。

❸ 这个软件是我打开的。

连词成句。Connect the words into sentences.

❶ 3D打印　人造骨粉　研发　是　针对　设备　的

_____

❷ 这　哪儿　个　创建　文件　是　在　的

_____

❸ 文件　转换　格式　你　是　的　吗

_____

❹ 这些　针对　打印　研发　材料　工艺　是　3D　的

_____

第 13 课 | 打印材料

汉字书写 Writing Chinese Characters

rén
人 人 人
人 人 人 人 人

shēng
生 生 生 生 生
生 生 生 生 生

zhǔ
主 主 主 主 主
主 主 主 主 主

yì
艺 艺 艺 艺
艺 艺 艺 艺 艺

文化拓展 Culture Insight

The compass, known as *sinan* in ancient times, is a result of the ancient Chinese laborers' long-term practice and understanding of magnetic properties. It stands as one of the Four Great Inventions of ancient China.  Its primary component is a magnetic needle mounted on a shaft, which can freely rotate under the influence of the Earth's natural magnetic field and align itself with the tangential direction of the magnetic meridian. This functionality allows it to determine directions. Its invention has played an immeasurable role in advancing human science, technology, and civilization.

123

小结 Summary

1. 听句子选词填空。Listen to the sentences and choose the words to fill in the blanks. 🎧 13-03

> A. 形态　　　B. 领域　　　C. 陶瓷　　　D. 研发

❶ 生物_____使用的材料有人造骨粉、生物原料等。

❷ 3D 打印使用的材料有塑料、光敏树脂、石膏、金属和_____等。

❸ 这些材料是针对 3D 打印设备和工艺_____的。

❹ 材料有不同的_____，例如粉末、丝状、液体等。

2. 看词语练拼音。Look at the words and practice Pinyin.

| guāngmǐn | táocí | shēngwù | yuánliào |
| 光敏 | 陶瓷 | 生物 | 原料 |

| bù tóng | xíngtài | zhēnduì | shígāo |
| 不同 | 形态 | 针对 | 石膏 |

3. 朗读下列句子。Read aloud the following sentences.

❶ 3D dǎyìn shǐyòng de cáiliào yǒu sùliào、guāngmǐn shùzhī、shígāo、jīnshǔ hé táocí děng.
　3D 打印使用的材料有塑料、光敏树脂、石膏、金属和陶瓷等。

❷ Shēngwù lǐngyù shǐyòng de cáiliào yǒu rénzào gǔfěn、shēngwù yuánliào děng.
　生物领域使用的材料有人造骨粉、生物原料等。

第14课 识别激光器
Lesson 14 Identifying Lasers

Shíbié jīguāngqì

 复习 Revision

1. 根据图片选择词语。 Choose the words based on the pictures.

❶ 陶瓷（　　）　　❷ 金属（　　）　　❸ 研发（　　）
　 塑料（　　）　　　 石膏（　　）　　　 喷绘（　　）

2. 把下列词语组合成短语或句子。 Connect the words into phrases or sentences.

❶ ①不同的　②有　③形态　④材料

_____

❷ ①材料　②有　③塑料　④使用的

_____

3 ①领域　　②生物　　③有　　④人造骨粉　　⑤使用的　　⑥材料

热身 Warm-up

你认识这些词语吗？ Do you know these words?

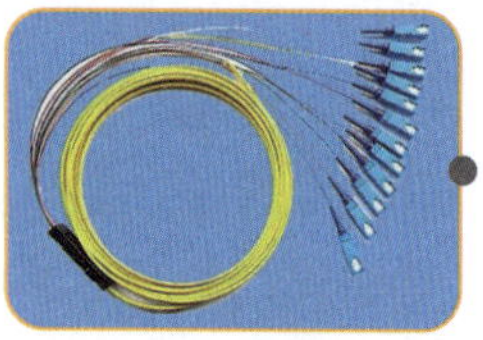 光纤图	guāngxiān 光纤	optical fiber
 拼图	pǐpèi 匹配	match
 激光器图	jīguāngqì 激光器	laser (device)
 包含圆环图	bāokuò 包括	include
 火箭发射图	fāshè 发射	emit
 建筑顶部图	dǐngbù 顶部	top

学习生词 Words and Expressions 🎧 14-01

1	识别	shíbié	v.	identify
2	激光器	jīguāngqì	n.	laser (device)
3	发射	fāshè	v.	emit
4	源泉	yuánquán	n.	source
5	一般	yìbān	adv.	usually
6	顶部	dǐngbù	n.	top
7	精密	jīngmì	adj.	precise
8	核心	héxīn	n.	core
9	器件	qìjiàn	n.	device
10	主流	zhǔliú	n.	mainstream
11	包括	bāokuò	v.	include
12	紫外激光器	zǐwài jīguāngqì	phr.	ultraviolet laser
13	光纤激光器	guāngxiān jīguāngqì	phr.	fiber laser
14	根据	gēnjù	prep.	according to
15	匹配	pǐpèi	v.	match

词语练习 Word Exercises

1. 学习词语搭配。Study the collocations.

❶ héxīn 核心	héxīn qìjiàn 核心 器件	core component
	héxīn jìshù 核心 技术	core technology
❷ dǐngbù 顶部	shèbèi dǐngbù 设备 顶部	top of the equipment
	dǐngbù shèjì 顶部 设计	top design
❸ pǐpèi 匹配	pǐpèi cáiliào 匹配 材料	match the materials
	pǐpèi jīqì 匹配 机器	match the machines

2. 给词语选择正确搭配。Choose the right words to form collocations.

❶ _____ jīguāngqì 激光器   A. héxīn 核心   B. shíbié 识别

❷ néngliàng 能量_____   A. yuánquán 源泉   B. dǎkāi 打开

❸ fāshè 发射_____   A. wèizhì 位置   B. jīguāng 激光

第14课 | 识别激光器

 **学习课文 Text** 🎧 14-02

激光器发射的激光是材料成型的能量源泉,它的位置一般在设备顶部,可以通过软件控制,是3D打印机最精密的核心器件。主流激光器包括紫外激光器、光纤激光器和CO_2激光器等,3D打印机根据成型材料的不同匹配不同的激光器。

The laser emitted by the laser device is the energy source for material forming. It is typically located at the top of the equipment and can be controlled via software, making it the most precise core component of a 3D printer. Mainstream lasers include ultraviolet lasers, fiber lasers, and CO_2 lasers. 3D printers match different lasers according to the materials used for molding.

129

课文练习 Text Exercises

1. 回答问题。Answer the questions.

① 激光器发射的什么是材料成型的能量源泉？

② 激光器的位置一般在设备底部吗？

2. 根据课文选词填空。Choose the words to fill in the blanks based on the text.

A. 精密　　B. 光纤　　C. 源泉　　D. 匹配

① 激光器是3D打印机最_____的核心器件。

② 3D打印机根据成型材料的不同_____不同的激光器。

学习语法 Grammar

 语法点1 Grammar Point 1

副词"最"　The adverb "最"

It is used before an adjective to indicate that the degree of a certain nature or state outperforms that of similar things.

① 激光器是3D打印机中最精密的核心器件。

② 这个模型的外壳最厚。

③ 谁的中文最好？

连词成句。Connect the words into sentences.

1. 激光器　器件　是　精密　3D打印机　核心　中　最　的

_____

2. 哪　个　步骤　最　重要

_____

3. 这　文件　的　个　新　是　最

_____

4. 发音　我　最　的　好

_____

语法点 2 Grammar Point 2

介词"根据"　The preposition "根据"

It is used to introduce the basis of an action or a behavior. The common structure is: 按照 + noun + verbal phrase.

1. 3D打印机根据成型材料的不同匹配不同的激光器。
2. 根据不同的需要，选择不同功能模块。
3. 请根据这五个步骤进行操作。

选词填空。Choose the words to fill in the blanks.

A. 根据　　B. 通过

1. 三维激光扫描技术可以_____获取被测物体表面大量密集的数据信息，快速建立三维模型。

2. 模型可以_____添加支撑，防止变形。

3. 3D打印机_____成型材料的不同匹配不同的激光器。

4. _____不同的需要，选择不同功能模块。

 ## 汉字书写 Writing Chinese Characters

le	了 了
fā	发 发 发 发 发
zhōng	中 中 中 中
xīn	心 心 心 心

 ## 职业拓展 Career Insight

Mainstream laser sintering 3D printing utilizes carbon dioxide lasers because polymer materials exhibit higher absorption rates for lasers within the 10.6 μm wavelength band. To further enhance forming efficiency, additional components are often added to the materials to increase their laser absorption.

第14课 | 识别激光器

 **小结 Summary**

1. 听句子选词填空。Listen to the sentences and choose the words to fill in the blanks. 🎧 14-03

> A. 包括　　　B. 激光器　　　C. 匹配　　　D. 顶部

① _____可以通过软件控制。

② 激光器的位置一般在设备_____。

③ 主流激光器_____紫外激光器、光纤激光器和CO_2激光器等。

④ 3D打印机根据成型材料的不同_____不同的激光器。

2. 看词语练拼音。Look at the words and practice Pinyin.

shíbié	jīguāngqì	fāshè	yuánquán
识别	激光器	发射	源泉
jīngmì	héxīn	qìjiàn	gēnjù
精密	核心	器件	根据

3. 朗读下列句子。Read aloud the following sentences.

① Jīguāngqì fāshè de jīguāng shì cáiliào chéngxíng de néngliàng yuánquán.
　　激光器 发射 的 激光 是 材料 成型 的 能量 源泉。

② Zhǔliú jīguāngqì bāokuò zǐwài jīguāngqì、guāngxiān jīguāngqì hé CO_2 jīguāngqì děng.
　　主流 激光器 包括 紫外 激光器、光纤 激光器 和 CO_2激光器 等。

第15课 Lesson 15
操作水冷机
Cāozuò shuǐlěngjī
Operating Water Chillers

 复习 Revision

1. 根据图片选择词语。Choose the words based on the pictures.

❶ 激光器（　　）　　❷ 识别（　　）　　❸ 匹配（　　）
　 光纤（　　）　　　　 发射（　　）　　　 主流（　　）

2. 把下列词语组合成短语或句子。Connect the words into phrases or sentences.

❶ ①通过　　②软件　　③控制　　④可以

_____

❷ ①精密的　　②器件　　③核心　　④最

_____

第15课 | 操作水冷机

3 ①材料　②根据　③激光器　④匹配

_____

 热身 Warm-up

你认识这些词语吗？ Do you know these words?

　　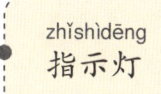 zhǐshìdēng 指示灯　　indicator light

　　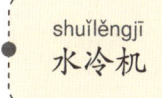 shuǐlěngjī 水冷机　　water chiller

　　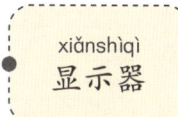 xiǎnshìqì 显示器　　display

　　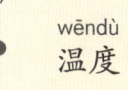 wēndù 温度　　temperature

　　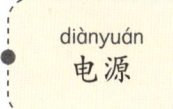 diànyuán 电源　　power supply

　　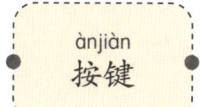 ànjiàn 按键　　button

135

学习生词 Words and Expressions  15-01

1	操作	cāozuò	v.	operate
2	水冷机	shuǐlěngjī	n.	water chiller
3	先	xiān	adv.	first
4	电源	diànyuán	n.	power supply
5	指示灯	zhǐshìdēng	n.	indicator light
6	变亮	biànliàng	phr.	be turned on
7	按键	ànjiàn	n.	button
8	通电	tōng//diàn	v.	power up
9	显示器	xiǎnshìqì	n.	display
10	温度	wēndù	n.	temperature
11	设置	shèzhì	v.	set, configure
12	运转	yùnzhuǎn	v.	run, operate
13	正常	zhèngcháng	adj.	normal
14	关闭	guānbì	v.	close, shut down, turn off
15	相反	xiāngfǎn	adj.	reverse, opposite

第15课 | 操作水冷机

 词语练习 Word Exercises

1. 学习词语搭配。Study the collocations.

① shèzhì 设置	shèzhì wēndù 设置 温度	set the temperature
	shèzhì cānshù 设置 参数	set the parameters
② yùnzhuǎn 运转	jīqì yùnzhuǎn 机器 运转	machine operation
	shèbèi yùnzhuǎn 设备 运转	equipment operation
③ cāozuò 操作	cāozuò shèbèi 操作 设备	operate the equipment
	cāozuò jīqì 操作 机器	operate the machine

2. 给词语选择正确搭配。Choose the right words to form collocations.

① shèzhì
设置_____   A. cānshù 参数   B. ànjiàn 按键

② yùnzhuǎn
运转_____   A. xiāngfǎn 相反   B. zhèngcháng 正常

③ cāozuò
操作_____   A. bùzhòu 步骤   B. wēndù 温度

137

学习课文 Text 🎧 15-02

第一步：打开激光器前，先打开水冷机电源。

第二步：电源指示灯变亮，按下控制按键，机器控制系统通电，显示器变亮。

第三步：水冷机控制温度一般设置在22℃左右。

第四步：在水冷机运转正常之后，才可以打开激光器。

第五步：关闭步骤和打开步骤相反。

Step 1: Before turning on the laser, first switch on the power of the water chiller.

Step 2: When the power indicator light is on, turn on the control button to power up the control system of the machine, and the display will be turned on.

Step 3: The control temperature of the water chiller is generally set at around 22 ℃.

Step 4: Only after the water chiller is operating normally can the laser be turned on.

Step 5: The procedure for turning off is the reverse of the procedure for turning on.

课文练习 Text Exercises

1. 回答问题。Answer the questions.

① 先打开激光器还是先打开水冷机电源？

② 水冷机控制温度一般设置为 22 ℃ 吗？

2. 根据课文选词填空。Choose the words to fill in the blanks based on the text.

| A. 设置 | B. 运转 | C. 按下 | D. 关闭 |

① 电源指示灯变亮，_____控制按键。

② 在水冷机_____正常之后，才可以打开激光器。

学习语法 Grammar

语法点 1　Grammar Point 1

方位词"左右"　The word of location "左右"

　　It is used after a measure word to indicate slightly more or less than this quantity.

1. 水冷机控制温度一般设置在 22 ℃ 左右。
2. 光固化成型需要 5 个左右的步骤。
3. 今天学习的生词有 20 个左右。

选词填空。Choose the words to fill in the blanks.

1. 水冷机控制温度一般设置在_____。（左右　22 ℃）
2. 我_____去上课。（7:30　左右）
3. 激光成型需要_____。（5　左右　个　步骤）
4. 这本书有_____。（左右　200 页）

语法点 2　Grammar Point 2

只有……，才……　only when..., can...

　　It indicates a necessary and the only condition.

1. 只有在水冷机运转正常之后，才可以打开激光器。
2. 只有把模型文件格式转换为 STL 格式以后，才可以对模型进行打印。
3. 只有加入原料以后，才可以开始打印。

句子连线。**Match the parts of the sentences.**

1. 只有在水冷机运转正常之后， 才可以开始打印。
2. 只有把模型文件格式转换为 STL 格式以后， 才可以打开激光器。
3. 只有加入原料后， 才可以建立三维模型。
4. 只有获取被测物体表面信息， 才可以对模型进行打印。

汉字书写 Writing Chinese Characters

职业拓展 Career Insight

Movable type printing is an ancient printing technique and one of the Four Great Inventions of ancient China. It was invented by ancient Chinese laborers through persistent practice and research. The process begins with creating reverse matrices for raised Chinese characters, followed by selecting these characters based on the manuscript. These characters are then arranged on character plates and inked for printing. After printing, the matrices are removed for reuse in subsequent typesetting and printing. The invention of movable type printing marked a significant technological revolution in the history of printing.

小结 Summary

1. 听句子选词填空。Listen to the sentences and choose the words to fill in the blanks. 15-03

   A. 按键　　　B. 电源　　　C. 运转　　　D. 温度

   ❶ 在操作水冷机的过程中，只有在水冷机_____正常之后，才可以打开激光器。

   ❷ 按下控制_____，机器控制系统通电。

第15课 | 操作水冷机

3 水冷机控制_____一般设置在 22 ℃ 左右。

4 水冷机操作第一步,先打开水冷机_____开关。

2. 看词语练拼音。Look at the words and practice Pinyin.

ànjiàn　　　　shèzhì　　　　tōngdiàn　　　　zhǐshìdēng
按键　　　　　设置　　　　　通电　　　　　　指示灯

zhèngcháng　　guānbì　　　　wēndù　　　　　shuǐlěngjī
正常　　　　　关闭　　　　　温度　　　　　　水冷机

3. 朗读下列句子。Read aloud the following sentences.

1 Shuǐlěngjī kòngzhì wēndù yìbān shèzhì zài 22 ℃ zuǒyòu.
  水冷机 控制 温度一般 设置 在 22 ℃ 左右。

2 Zài shuǐlěngjī yùnzhuǎn zhèngcháng zhīhòu, cái kěyǐ dǎkāi jīguāngqì.
  在 水冷机 运转 正常 之后,才 可以 打开 激光器。

第16课 Lesson 16

Tiānjiā yuánliào
添加原料
Adding Raw Materials

 复习 Revision

1. 根据图片选择词语。 Choose the words based on the pictures.

❶ 显示器（　　）　　❷ 基板（　　　）　　❸ 按下（　　　）
　 图形（　　）　　　 水冷机（　　）　　 铺平（　　　）

2. 把下列词语组合成短语或句子。 Connect the words into phrases or sentences.

❶ ①电源　　②打开　　③开关　　④水冷机

_____

❷ ①按下　　②开关　　③再　　　④控制

_____

144

第16课 | 添加原料

3 ①系统　②机器　③通电　④控制

 热身 Warm-up

你认识这些词语吗？ Do you know these words?

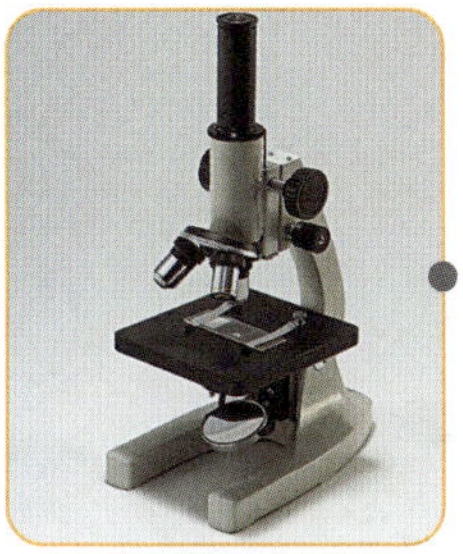

显微镜 xiǎnwēijìng		microscope
颗粒 kēlì		particle
螺钉 luódīng		screw
工具 gōngjù		tool
检测 jiǎncè		detect
氧化 yǎnghuà		oxidize

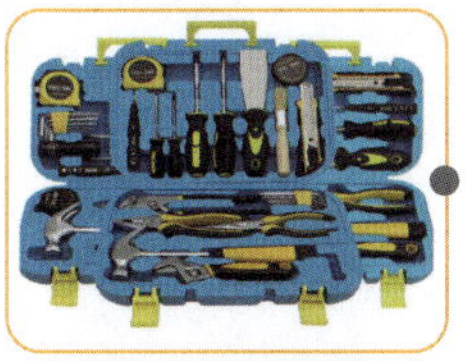

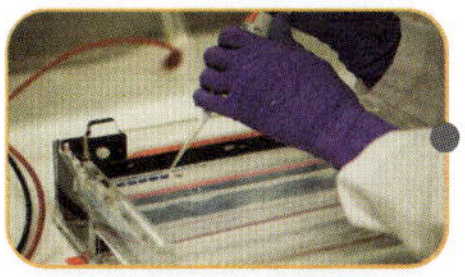

145

学习生词 Words and Expressions 16-01

1	保证	bǎozhèng	v.	ensure
2	干燥	gānzào	adj.	dry
3	避免	bìmiǎn	v.	avoid
4	氧化	yǎnghuà	v.	oxidize
5	光学	guāngxué	n.	optics
6	显微镜	xiǎnwēijìng	n.	microscope
7	检测	jiǎncè	v.	detect
8	颗粒	kēlì	n.	particle
9	粒径	lìjìng	n.	particle size
10	分布	fēnbù	v.	distribute
11	工具	gōngjù	n.	tool
12	查看	jiǎnchá	v.	check
13	是否	shìfǒu	adv.	whether or not
14	遗落	yíluò	v.	leave behind
15	螺钉	luódīng	n.	screw
16	均匀	jūnyún	adj.	uniform, even

第16课 | 添加原料

词语练习 Word Exercises

1. 学习词语搭配。Study the collocations.

❶ chákàn 查看	chákàn xìnxī 查看 信息	check the information
	chákàn shùjù 查看 数据	check the data
❷ bǎozhèng 保证	bǎozhèng ānquán 保证 安全	ensure the safety
	zhìliàng bǎozhèng 质量 保证	quality assurance
❸ fēnbù 分布	jūnyún fēnbù 均匀 分布	uniform distribution
	mìjí fēnbù 密集 分布	dense distribution

2. 给词语选择正确搭配。Choose the right words to form collocations.

❶ tiānjiā 添加_____　A. zhìpǐn 制品　B. fěnmò 粉末

❷ bìmiǎn 避免_____　A. yǎnghuà 氧化　B. shēngchéng 生成

❸ jūnyún 均匀_____　A. fěnmò 粉末　B. pūpíng 铺平

147

学习课文 Text 🎧 16-02

第一步：保证添加的粉末是干燥的，并避免氧化。

第二步：在光学显微镜下检测粉末颗粒的粒径分布。

第三步：通过工具添加粉末，并保证粉末顶部是铺平的。

第四步：查看粉末内是否遗落螺钉等物体。

第五步：保证第一层粉末是均匀的和铺平的。

Step 1: Ensure that the powder to be added is dry and avoid oxidation.

Step 2: Detect the particle size distribution of powder particles under an optical microscope.

第 16 课 | 添加原料

Step 3: Add powder using tools and ensure that the top of the powder is leveled.

Step 4: Check if any objects such as screws are left in the powder.

Step 5: Ensure that the first layer of powder is uniform and leveled.

课文练习 Text Exercises

1. 回答问题。Answer the questions.

① 添加的粉末是干燥的吗？

② 在光学显微镜下可以观察到粉末颗粒的粒径分布情况吗？

2. 根据课文选词填空。Choose the words to fill in the blanks based on the text.

> A. 可以　　　B. 遗落　　　C. 均匀　　　D. 会

① 查看粉末内是否_____螺钉等物体。

② 保证第一层粉末是_____的和铺平的。

学习语法 Grammar

语法点 1　Grammar Point 1

> **方位词 "内"　The word of location "内"**
>
> "内" is used after a noun to indicate the interior of an object. "里" is often used in spoken Chinese instead.
>
> ❶ 检查粉末内是否遗落螺钉等物体。
>
> ❷ 在电脑内用软件建立模型。
>
> ❸ 请确保设备内是干燥的。

选词填空。Choose the words to fill in the blanks.

A. 内　　　B. 向

❶ 检查粉末_____是否遗落螺钉等物体。

❷ _____设备加入金属粉末。

❸ 在电脑_____用软件建立模型。

❹ _____切片软件导入模型。

语法点 2　Grammar Point 2

副词"是否"　The adverb "是否"

It means "whether... or not" and is often used in written Chinese. The structure is: subject + 是否 + predicate.

1. 检查粉末内是否遗落螺钉等物体。
2. 是否需要对文件格式进行转换？
3. 热塑性材料是否加热到液体状态了？

连词成句。Connect the words into sentences.

1. 内　　遗漏　　粉末　　是否　　螺钉

   _____

2. 请　　格式　　检查　　转换　　文件　　是否　　了

   _____

3. 是否　　需要　　加热　　把　　到　　材料　　液体　　状态

   _____

4. 3D打印　　可以　　是否　　用　　工业　　在　　领域

   _____

汉字书写 Writing Chinese Characters

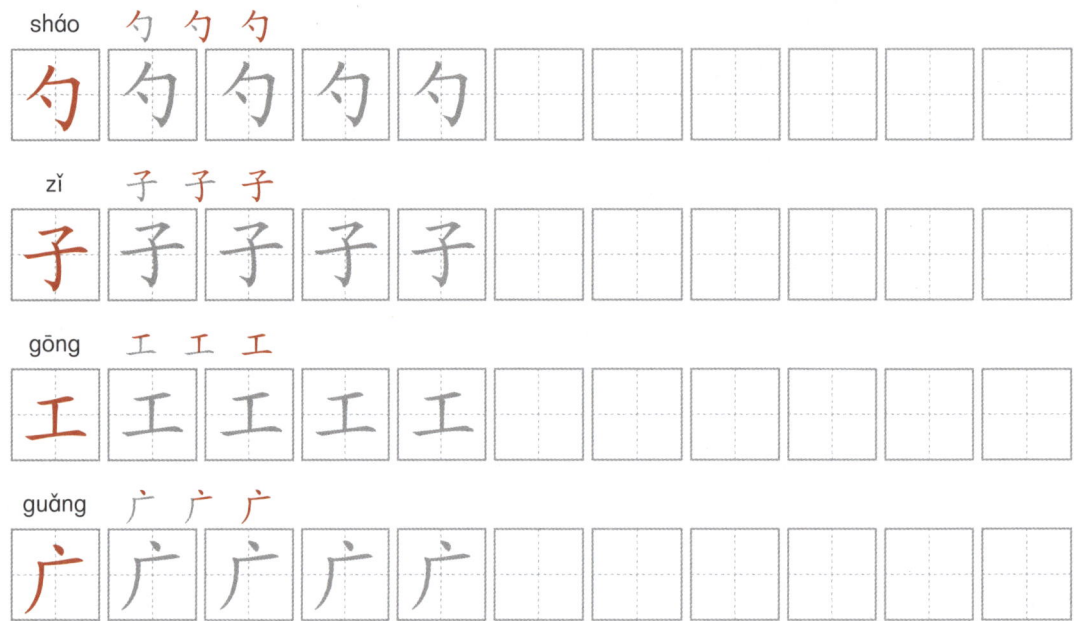

职业拓展 Career Insight

As the maturity and performance of 3D printing technology continue to advance, the range of materials suitable for 3D printing is expanding significantly, particularly in the realm of metal materials. Metal 3D printing technology, recognized as the most cutting-edge and promising within the 3D printing system, represents a crucial direction in advanced manufacturing technology.

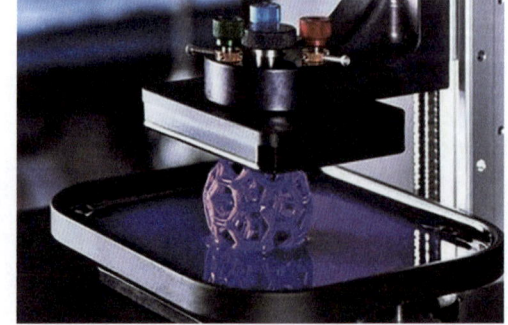

小结 Summary

1. 听句子选词填空。Listen to the sentences and choose the words to fill in the blanks. 🎧 16-03

> A. 粉末　　　B. 光学　　　C. 颗粒　　　D. 工具

① 在添加粉末时，要用专用_____添加适量粉末至机器粉末槽内。

② 通常情况下，在_____显微镜下可以清楚地观察粉末的组织结构。

③ 粉末冶金高温材料包括_____冶金高温合金、难熔金属和合金、金属陶瓷、弥散强化和纤维强化材料等。

④ 用小勺子的柄轻轻地在粉槽内左右搅动一下，以确保粉末里面没有掺杂杂质_____。

2. 看词语练拼音。Look at the words and practice Pinyin.

bìmiǎn	bǎozhèng	guānchá	jiǎnchá
避免	保证	观察	检查

yídòng	dǐngbù	gōngjù	guāngxué
移动	顶部	工具	光学

3. 朗读下列句子。Read aloud the following sentences.

① Tiānjiā de fěnmò bìxū shì gānzào de, bìng bìmiǎn yǎnghuà.
　 添加的粉末必须是干燥的，并避免氧化。

② Kěyǐ zài guāngxué xiǎnwēijìng xià guānchá fěnmò kēlì de lìjìng fēnbù qíngkuàng.
　 可以在光学显微镜下观察粉末颗粒的粒径分布情况。

第17课 Lesson 17

操作软件 Cāozuò ruǎnjiàn
Operating Software

 复习 Revision

1. 根据图片选择词语。Choose the words based on the pictures.

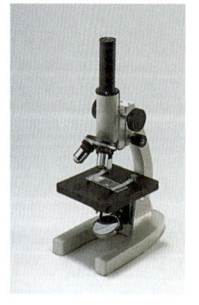  

❶ 显微镜（　　　）　　❷ 螺钉（　　　）　　❸ 粉末（　　　）
　 显示器（　　　）　　　 位置（　　　）　　　 颗粒（　　　）

2. 把下列词语组合成短语或句子。Connect the words into phrases or sentences.

1　①粉末　　②干燥的　　③保证　　④是

_____

2　①观察　　②分布　　③情况　　④粒径

_____

第17课 | 操作软件

3 ①工具　②添加　③通过　④粉末

 ## 热身 Warm-up

你认识这些词语吗？ Do you know these words?

 速度表图	sùdù 速度	speed
 加工图	jiāgōng 加工	process
 观察图	guānchá 观察	observe
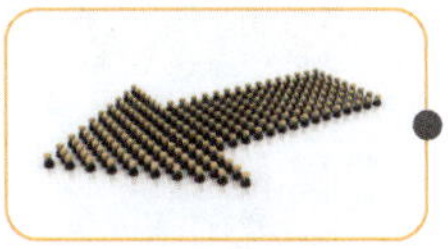 数量图	shùliàng 数量	quantity
 多层建筑图	duōcéng 多层	multi-layer
 功率表图	gōnglǜ 功率	power

155

 学习生词 Words and Expressions 🎧 17-01

1	配套	pèi//tào	v.	(be) matching, (be) supporting
2	反转	fǎnzhuǎn	v.	reverse
3	需求	xūqiú	n.	requirement
4	调整	tiáozhěng	v.	adjust
5	数量	shùliàng	n.	quantity
6	速度	sùdù	n.	speed
7	次数	cìshù	n.	number of times, frequency
8	功率	gōnglǜ	n.	power
9	延时	yánshí	n.	delay
10	加工	jiā//gōng	v.	process
11	同时	tóngshí	conj.	at the same time
12	观察	guānchá	v.	observe
13	如果	rúguǒ	conj.	if, whether
14	后续	hòuxù	adj.	subsequent
15	多层	duōcéng	adj.	multi-layer

第 17 课 | 操作软件

词语练习 Word Exercises

1. 学习词语搭配。Study the collocations.

❶ tiáozhěng 调整	tiáozhěng shùliàng 调整 数量	adjust the quantity
	tiáozhěng gōnglǜ 调整 功率	adjust the power
❷ sùdù 速度	shèdìng sùdù 设定 速度	set the speed
	tiáozhěng sùdù 调整 速度	adjust the speed
❸ jiāgōng 加工	zhèngcháng jiāgōng 正常 加工	normal processing
	wánchéng jiāgōng 完成 加工	complete the processing

2. 给词语选择正确搭配。Choose the right words to form collocations.

❶ tiáozhěng
调整＿＿＿＿＿ A. shùliàng 数量   B. túxíng 图形

❷ duōcéng
多层＿＿＿＿＿ A. ruǎnjiàn 软件   B. dǎyìn 打印

❸ fǎnzhuǎn
反转＿＿＿＿＿ A. xuǎnzé 选择   B. móxíng 模型

157

 学习课文 Text 🎧 17-02

第一步：向设备配套软件导入模型文件。

第二步：在软件中移动、反转模型，根据需求调整数量、位置并添加支撑。

第三步：设定扫描速度、次数、移动速度、激光功率、延时等参数。

第四步：进行第一层加工，同时观察是否正常。

第五步：如果加工正常，就进行后续多层打印。

第 17 课 | 操作软件

Step 1: Import the model file into the supporting software of the device.

Step 2: Move and reverse the model in the software, adjust the quantity and position according to the requirements, and add support.

Step 3: Set parameters such as scanning speed, frequency, movement speed, laser power, delay, etc.

Step 4: Perform the first-layer processing and meanwhile observe whether it is normal.

Step 5: If the processing is normal, perform the subsequent multi-layer printing.

课文练习 Text Exercises

1. 回答问题。Answer the questions.

① 需要向设备软件中导入模型文件吗？

② 第二层加工正常后，进行后续多层制造吗？

2. 根据课文选词填空。Choose the words to fill in the blanks based on the text.

A. 需求　　　B. 导入　　　C. 进行　　　D. 设定

① 在设备软件中移动零件三维模型，根据打印_____调整参数及添加支撑。

② 在设备软件中_____扫描速度、移动速度、激光功率等打印参数。

159

 学习语法 Grammar

 语法点 1　Grammar Point 1

连词"同时" The conjunction "同时"

　　It indicates a parallel relationship and often means the advancement to the next level. The common structure is: ……, 同时 + verbal phrase.

❶ 进行第一层加工，同时观察打印是否正常。

❷ 导入 3D 模型，同时设定打印参数。

❸ 检查文件格式，同时修复 STL 文件。

选词填空。Choose the words to fill in the blanks.

A. 的时候　　　B. 同时

❶ 进行第一层加工，_____观察打印是否正常。

❷ 导入 3D 模型，_____设定打印参数。

❸ 操作切片软件_____，需要设定哪些参数？

❹ 打印第一层_____，需要观察打印是否正常。

 语法点 2　Grammar Point 2

如果……，就…… if..., then...

　　It indicates a hypothetical conditional relationships.

1. 如果第一层加工正常，就进行后续多层打印。
2. 如果水冷机运转正常，就可以打开激光器。
3. 如果零件打印完成了，就需要进行表面清理。

选词填空。Choose the words to fill in the blanks.

A. 如果   B. 只有

1. _____ 第一层加工正常，就进行后续多层打印。
2. _____ 水冷机运转正常，就可以打开激光器。
3. _____ 在水冷机运转正常之后，才可以打开激光器。
4. _____ 把模型文件格式转换为STL以后，才可以对模型进行软件切片。

汉字书写 Writing Chinese Characters

chū
出 出 出 出 出 出

bù
步 步 步 步 步 步

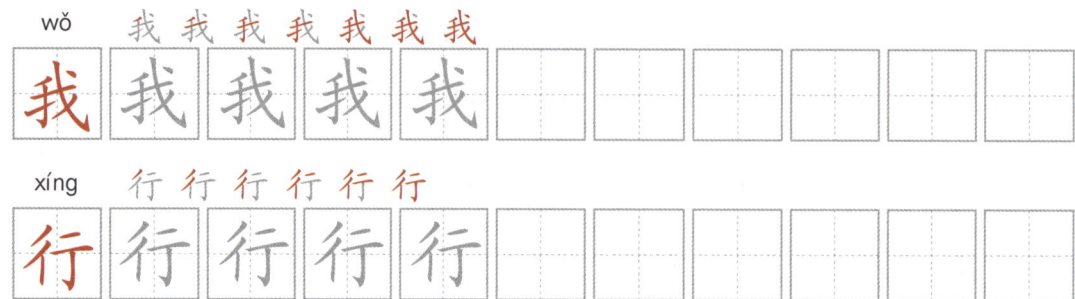

 文化拓展 Culture Insight

Gunpowder, also known as black powder, is a mechanical mixture of potassium nitrate, charcoal, and sulfur. It stands as one of China's Four Great Inventions and is the result of the persistent practice of Chinese alchemy and pharmacy, boasting a history of over a thousand years. As an outstanding achievement in the history of human civilization, gunpowder has significantly propelled societal and civilizational development, fostering global cultural exchange and integration.

第 17 课 | 操作软件

 小结 Summary

1. 听句子选词填空。Listen to the sentences and choose the words to fill in the blanks. 🎧 17-03

> A. 加工　　　B. 配套　　　C. 观察　　　D. 调整

❶ 同时_____是否正常。

❷ 进行第一层_____。

❸ 根据需求_____数量。

❹ 向设备_____软件中导入模型。

2. 看词语练拼音。Look at the words and practice Pinyin.

guānchá	hòuxù	shùliàng	duōcéng
观察	后续	数量	多层
tóngshí	sùdù	cìshù	jiāgōng
同时	速度	次数	加工

3. 朗读下列句子。Read aloud the following sentences.

❶ Xiàng shèbèi pèitào ruǎnjiàn dǎorù móxíng wénjiàn.
   向 设备 配套 软件 导入 模型 文件。

❷ Rúguǒ jiāgōng zhèngcháng, jiù jìnxíng hòuxù duōcéng dǎyìn.
   如果 加工 正常，就 进行 后续 多层 打印。

163

第18课 Lesson 18

Jiǎnchá shèbèi
检查设备
Checking Equipment

 复习 Revision

1. 根据图片选择词语。Choose the words based on the pictures.

❶ 加工（   ）　　❷ 功率（   ）　　❸ 影像（   ）
　扫描（   ）　　　加热（   ）　　　速度（   ）

2. 把下列词语组合成短语或句子。Connect the words into phrases or sentences.

① ①观察　②打印　③正常　④是否

_____

② ①零件　②模型　③移动　④三维

_____

3. ①设备　②设定　③软件　④参数

_____

热身 Warm-up

你认识这些词语吗？ Do you know these words?

	diànxiàn 电线	electric wire
	qìyā 气压	air pressure
	jiāoquān 胶圈	rubber ring
	máoshuā 毛刷	brush
	guǎndào 管道	pipeline
	tōngfēng 通风	ventilate

165

学习生词 Words and Expressions 🎧 18-01

1	电线	diànxiàn	n.	electric wire
2	管道	guǎndào	n.	pipeline
3	气压	qìyā	n.	air pressure
4	大于	dàyú	v.	be greater than
5	等于	děngyú	v.	be equal to
6	外观	wàiguān	n.	appearance
7	脱落	tuōluò	v.	detach
8	移位	yí//wèi	v.	displace
9	密封	mìfēng	v.	seal
10	胶圈	jiāoquān	n.	rubber ring
11	完整	wánzhěng	adj.	intact
12	毛刷	máoshuā	n.	brush
13	环境	huánjìng	n.	environment
14	通风	tōng//fēng	v.	ventilate
15	措施	cuòshī	n.	measure

第18课 | 检查设备

词语练习 Word Exercises

1. 学习词语搭配。Study the collocations.

huánjìng ❶ 环境	gōngzuò huánjìng 工作 环境	work environment
	gōngyè huánjìng 工业 环境	industrial environment
qìyā ❷ 气压	jiǎnchá qìyā 检查 气压	check the air pressure
	qìyā zhèngcháng 气压 正常	normal air pressure
tōngfēng ❸ 通风	tōngfēng cuòshī 通风 措施	ventilation measures
	tōngfēng zhèngcháng 通风 正常	normal ventilation

2. 给词语选择正确搭配。Choose the right words to form collocations.

gōngzuò
❶ 工作_____
       huánjìng   túxíng
    A. 环境   B. 图形

mìfēng
❷ 密封_____
       jiāoquān   duì de
    A. 胶圈   B. 对的

tōngfēng
❸ 通风_____
       xuǎnzé   cuòshī
    A. 选择   B. 措施

学习课文 Text 🎧 18-02

第一步：检查设备、连接电线和管道等是否正常。

第二步：检查气压是否大于等于 2 MPa。

第三步：检查外观是否变形，激光设备是否脱落或移位，密封胶圈是否完整。

第四步：检查是否遗落螺钉、工具、毛刷等。

第五步：检查工作环境是否有通风措施。

第18课 ｜ 检查设备

Step 1: Check whether the devices, connecting wires, and pipelines are normal.

Step 2: Check whether the air pressure is greater than or equal to 2 MPa.

Step 3: Check whether there is any deformation in the appearance, whether the laser device is detached or displaced, and whether the sealing rubber ring is intact.

Step 4: Check whether any screws, tools, brushes, etc. are left behind.

Step 5: Check whether there are ventilation measures in the working environment.

课文练习 Text Exercises

1. 回答问题。Answer the questions.

    ① 需要检查激光头是否脱落或移位吗？

    ② 工作环境需要有通风措施吗？

2. 根据课文选词填空。Choose the words to fill in the blanks based on the text.

    A. 移位   B. 操作   C. 通风   D. 变形

    ① 检查_____设备和电脑之间的电线和管道是否正常。

    ② 工作环境需要有_____措施。

学习语法 Grammar

语法点 1 Grammar Point 1

大于 / 高于 / 低于 / 大于等于 + 标准
greater than/higher than/lower than/greater than or equal to + standard

It indicates "exceeding".

1. 水冷机控制温度一般高于 20 ℃。
2. 气压低于 2 MPa 是不正常的。
3. 检查气压是否大于等于 2 MPa。

选词填空。Choose the words to fill in the blanks.

A. 对　　　B. 于

1. 水冷机控制温度一般高_____20 ℃。
2. _____模型进行软件切片。
3. 检查气压是否低_____2 MPa。
4. _____文件格式进行转换。

语法点 2 Grammar Point 2

连词 "或（或者）"　The conjunction "或（或者）"

It is used to indicate an alternative relationship. The common structure is: 或（或者）A 或（或者）B；A 或（或者）B。"或" is often used in written Chinese.

第18课 | 检查设备

1. 检查激光设备是否脱落或移位。
2. 3D打印的时候，我们需要使用树脂或者塑料等可黏合的材料。
3. 可以使用紫外激光器或者光纤激光器进行3D打印。

选词填空。Choose the words to fill in the blanks.

A. 或　　　　B. 并

1. 检查激光设备是否脱落_____移位。
2. 3D打印的时候，我们需要使用树脂_____塑料等可黏合的材料。
3. 检查_____修复STL文件。
4. 对模型进行软件切片_____添加支撑。

汉字书写 Writing Chinese Characters

qì
气 气 气 气 气
气 气 气 气 气

tóu
头 头 头 头 头 头
头 头 头 头 头

wèi
位 位 位 位 位 位 位
位 位 位 位 位

yǒu
有 有 有 有 有 有
有 有 有 有 有

171

职业拓展 Career Insight

Breakthroughs in technological processes will bring about improvements in efficiency. With the development of multi-laser printing devices in the additive manufacturing field, the printing efficiency of each additional laser head goes up by 20% – 50%. Compared with a four-laser-head device of the same volume, the printing efficiency of a six-laser-head device can be enhanced by about 30%.

小结 Summary

1. 听句子选词填空。Listen to the sentences and choose the words to fill in the blanks. 🎧 18-03

| A. 密封 | B. 措施 | C. 大于等于 | D. 脱落 |

❶ 检查_____胶圈是否完整。

❷ 检查保护气瓶的气压表读数是否_____2 MPa。

❸ 检查后部激光头是否_____。

4 工作环境需要有通风_____。

2. 看词语练拼音。Look at the words and practice Pinyin.

diànxiàn	bǎohù	guǎndào	wàiguān
电线	保护	管道	外观

biànxíng	jiāoquān	sōngdòng	máoshuā
变形	胶圈	松动	毛刷

3. 朗读下列句子。Read aloud the following sentences.

1 Jiǎnchá shìfǒu yǒu yíluò de luódīng、gōngjù、máoshuā děng wùtǐ.
检查 是否 有 遗落 的 螺钉、工具、毛刷 等 物体。

2 Jiǎnchá shìfǒu yíluò luódīng、gōngjù、máoshuā děng.
检查 是否 遗落 螺钉、工具、毛刷 等。

第19课 Lesson 19

启动设备 (Qǐdòng shèbèi)
Starting Equipment

 复习 Revision

1. 根据图片选择词语。Choose the words based on the pictures.

❶ 毛刷（　　）　　❷ 管道（　　　）　　❸ 胶圈（　　　）
　 橡胶（　　）　　　 电线（　　　）　　　 速度（　　　）

2. 把下列词语组合成短语或句子。Connect the words into phrases or sentences.

❶ ①检查　②读数　③气压表

_____

❷ ①外观　②是否　③检查　④变形

_____

❸ ①环境　②需要　③工作　④通风

_____

第 19 课 | 启动设备

 热身 Warm-up

你认识这些词语吗？ Do you know these words?

(按钮图)	qǐdòng 启动	start
(指示器图)	zhǐshìqì 指示器	indicator
(开关图)	kāiguān 开关	switch
(按下图)	ànxià 按下	press
(网线图)	wǎngxiàn 网线	network cable
(网络图)	wǎngluò 网络	network

175

学习生词 Words and Expressions 🎧 19-01

1	启动	qǐdòng	v.	start
2	提前	tíqián	v.	advance, bring forward
3	保持	bǎochí	v.	keep, maintain
4	下一步	xià yí bù	phr.	next step
5	指示器	zhǐshìqì	n.	indicator
6	出现	chūxiàn	v.	occur
7	异常	yìcháng	adj.	abnormal
8	情况	qíngkuàng	n.	situation
9	迅速	xùnsù	adj.	quick
10	按下	ànxia	phr.	press
11	急停	jítíng	phr.	emergency stop
12	开关	kāiguān	n.	switch
13	无法	wúfǎ	v.	be unable to
14	网线	wǎngxiàn	n.	network cable
15	网络	wǎngluò	n.	network
16	好	hǎo	adj.	well

第19课 | 启动设备

词语练习 Word Exercises

1. 学习词语搭配。Study the collocations.

kāiguān ① 开关	jítíng kāiguān 急停 开关	emergency stop switch
	diànyuán kāiguān 电源 开关	power switch
qǐdòng ② 启动	qǐdòng kāiguān 启动 开关	start the switch
	qǐdòng diànnǎo 启动 电脑	start the computer
qíngkuàng ③ 情况	jǐnjí qíngkuàng 紧急 情况	emergency
	zhèngcháng qíngkuàng 正常 情况	normal situation

2. 给词语选择正确搭配。Choose the right words to form collocations.

① qǐdòng 启动 _____   A. jìshù 技术   B. kāiguān 开关

② yìcháng 异常 _____   A. ruǎnjiàn 软件   B. qíngkuàng 情况

③ jítíng 急停 _____   A. kāiguān 开关   B. wénjiàn 文件

学习课文 Text 🎧 19-02

第一步：提前打开水冷机，使温度保持在22℃左右。

第二步：打开电源，观察机器指示灯是否变亮。

第三步：打开电脑，启动后进行下一步。

第四步：打开激光器，观察指示器是否正常，如果出现异常情况，迅速按下急停开关。

第五步：打开操作软件，如果无法打开，检查网线或者网络是否连接好。

第 19 课 | 启动设备

Step 1: Turn on the water chiller in advance to keep the temperature at around 22 °C.

Step 2: Turn on the power and observe whether the indicator light of the machine is on.

Step 3: Turn on the computer.

Step 4: Turn on the laser and observe whether the indicator is normal. If any abnormal situation occurs, quickly press the emergency stop switch.

Step 5: Open the operating software. If it cannot be opened, check whether the network cable or network is connected properly.

课文练习 Text Exercises

1. 回答问题。Answer the questions.

① 提前打开水冷机，温度需保持在多少度才能进行下一步操作？

② 打开主机电源，观看主机显示灯是否亮起，如果没有变化，需要检查吗？

③ 打开操作软件，如果提示控制系统无法打开，需要检查吗？

④ 操作软件如果无法打开，需要检查网线或者网络是否连接好了吗？

2. 根据课文选词填空。 Choose the words to fill in the blanks based on the text.

> A. 温度　　　　B. 开关　　　　C. 操作　　　　D. 检查

❶ 提前打开水冷机，待_____保持在22 ℃左右后，进行下一步。

❷ 打开_____软件。

❸ 如果系统无法打开，则需_____网线是否连接好。

❹ 打开激光器_____。

学习语法 Grammar

语法点 1　Grammar Point 1

用"使"的兼语句　Pivotal sentences with "使"

It indicates to cause a certain result to occur. The common structure is: 使 + noun + verbal/adjective phrase.

❶ 使温度保持在22 ℃左右。

❷ 我们需要使分层的厚度相等。

❸ 使热塑性材料凝固形成实物。

选词填空。Choose the words to fill in the blanks.

> A. 使　　　　B. 把

1. _____ 分层的厚度相等。
2. _____ 热塑性材料注入设备。
3. _____ 温度保持在 22 ℃ 左右。
4. 可以 _____ 增材制造技术用在工业领域。

语法点 2　Grammar Point 2

动词 + 好　Verb + 好

"好" is used after a verb to indicate that an action has been completed with a normal and satisfactory result.

1. 检查网线或者网络是否连接好。
2. 参数设定好了吗？
3. 请准备好打印材料。

连词成句。Connect the words into sentences.

1. 打印　模型　了　好

   _____

2. 请　打印　准备　材料　好

   _____

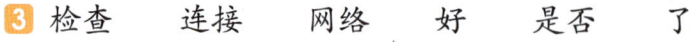

3 检查　连接　网络　好　是否　了

_____

4 请　设定　先　参数　好

_____

 汉字书写 Writing Chinese Characters

 文化拓展 Culture Insight

Dumplings (*jiaozi*) are a type of semicircular, cooked wheaten food wrapped in dumpling wrappers and filled with stuffing. Dumplings have a history of over 2,600 years. In 1972, several complete dumplings were unearthed from Tang Dynasty (618 A.D. – 907 A.D.) tombs in Turpan, Xinjiang. Dumplings can be cooked in various ways such as boiling, steaming, frying, grilling, etc. Since the Song Dynasty (960 A.D. – 1127 A.D.), dumplings have become a traditional festival food, usually eaten on the Winter Solstice. Since the Ming Dynasty (1368 A.D. – 1644 A.D.), there has been a custom of eating dumplings on the first day of the first lunar month.

 小结 Summary

1. 听句子选词填空。Listen to the sentences and choose the words to fill in the blanks. 19-03

| A. 启动 | B. 正常 | C. 急停 | D. 检查 |

❶ 打开电脑，并等待电脑_____后进入下一步。

2️⃣ 打开激光器开关,待激光器_____后进入下一步。

3️⃣ 打开操作软件,如果提示控制系统无法打开,则需_____网线是否连接好。

4️⃣ 观察主机指示灯是否变绿。如果没有变化,则检查_____按钮是否按下。

2. 看词语练拼音。**Look at the words and practice Pinyin.**

| jīguāng | ruǎnjiàn | jítíng | jiǎnchá |
| 激光 | 软件 | 急停 | 检查 |

| xiǎnshì | wǎngluò | zhǐshìdēng | cāozuò |
| 显示 | 网络 | 指示灯 | 操作 |

3. 朗读下列句子。**Read aloud the following sentences.**

1️⃣ Dǎkāi jīguāngqì, guānchá zhǐshìqì shìfǒu zhèngcháng.
打开 激光器,观察 指示器 是否 正常。

2️⃣ Dǎkāi diànyuán, guānchá jīqì zhǐshìdēng shìfǒu biànliàng.
打开 电源,观察 机器 指示灯 是否 变亮。

第20课 Lesson 20

操作设备 Cāozuò shèbèi
Operating Equipment

 **复习 Revision**

1. 根据图片选择词语。Choose the words based on the pictures.

❶ 启动（　　）　　❷ 开关（　　）　　❸ 制造（　　）
　模型（　　）　　　 技术（　　）　　　 网络（　　）

2. 把下列词语组合成短语或句子。Connect the words into phrases or sentences.

1 ①开关　②打开　③提前　④水冷机

_____

2 ①网络　②连接　③是否　④检查

_____

185

3. ①是否　②正常　③观察　④指示器

_____

热身 Warm-up

你认识这些词语吗？ Do you know these words?

 (缸体图)	gāngtǐ 缸体	cylinder block
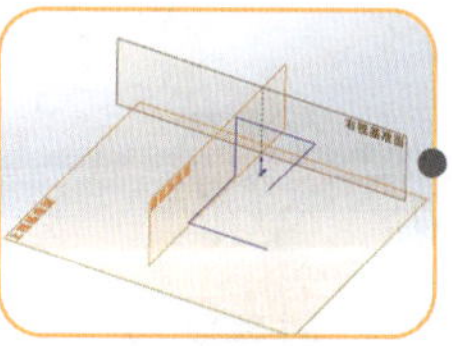 (基准面图)	jīzhǔnmiàn 基准面	datum plane
 (按钮图)	ànniǔ 按钮	button
 (存储器图)	cúnchǔqì 存储器	memory
 (计算机图)	jìsuànjī 计算机	computer
 (点击图)	diǎnjī 点击	click

第 20 课 | 操作设备

 学习生词 Words and Expressions  20-01

1	开机	kāi//jī	v.	(of a machine) be turned on
2	首先	shǒuxiān	adv.	first
3	调试	tiáoshì	v.	debug
4	对话框	duìhuàkuàng	n.	dialog box
5	然后	ránhòu	conj.	then
6	缸体	gāngtǐ	n.	cylinder block
7	底板	dǐbǎn	n.	base plate
8	上升	shàngshēng	v.	rise
9	基准面	jīzhǔnmiàn	n.	datum plane
10	安装	ānzhuāng	v.	install
11	点击	diǎnjī	v.	click
12	按钮	ànniǔ	n.	button
13	功能	gōngnéng	n.	function
14	存储器	cúnchǔqì	n.	memory
15	计算机	jìsuànjī	n.	computer

词语练习 Word Exercises

1. 学习词语搭配。Study the collocations.

❶ tiáoshì 调试	tiáoshì shèbèi 调试 设备	debug the equipment
	tiáoshì gāngtǐ 调试 缸体	debug the cylinder block
❷ ānzhuāng 安装	ānzhuāng jībǎn 安装 基板	install the base plate
	ānzhuāng shèbèi 安装 设备	install the equipment
❸ gōngnéng 功能	jiārè gōngnéng 加热 功能	heating function
	shàngshēng gōngnéng 上升 功能	rising function

2. 给词语选择正确搭配。Choose the right words to form collocations.

❶ ānzhuāng 安装 _____ A. duìhuàkuàng 对话框 B. jībǎn 基板

❷ shàngshēng 上升 _____ A. ruǎnjiàn 软件 B. jīzhǔnmiàn 基准面

❸ diǎnjī 点击 _____ A. ànniǔ 按钮 B. kāiguān 开关

学习课文 Text 🎧 20-02

第一步:开机后,首先打开"调试"对话框,然后调试缸体和铺粉系统。

第二步:把工作缸体底板上升到基准面,便于安装基板。

第三步:点击按钮,前后移动铺粉系统,观察是否正常。

第四步:根据需要打开加热功能。

第五步:通过存储器或网络把模型文件导入计算机,准备打印。

Step 1: After turning on the machine, first open the debugging dialog box, then debug the cylinder block and powder-spreading system.

Step 2: Raise the base plate of the working cylinder block to the datum plane to facilitate the installation of the substrate.

Step 3: Click the button to move the powder-spreading system back and forth, and observe whether it operates normally.

Step 4: Turn on the heating function as needed.

Step 5: Import the model file into the computer via the memory or network, and prepare for printing.

课文练习 Text Exercises

1. 回答问题。Answer the questions.

   ❶ 开机后是否先要调试缸体？

   ❷ 将底板上升到基准面以上是为了方便安装吗？

2. 根据课文选词填空。Choose the words to fill in the blanks based on the text.

   | A. 按钮 | B. 功能 | C. 对话框 | D. 和 |

   ❶ 打开"调试"_____。

   ❷ 根据需要打开加热_____。

学习语法 Grammar

语法点 1　Grammar Point 1

> 首先……，然后……　　first..., then...
>
> It is used to indicate the sequence of two actions or behaviors.
>
> ❶ 首先打开"调试"对话框，然后调试缸体和铺粉系统。
> ❷ 首先向设备加入金属粉末，然后用激光进行逐层扫描。
> ❸ 首先对模型进行软件切片，然后再添加支撑。

选词填空。Choose the words to fill in the blanks.

> A. 然后　　　　B. 后

❶ 金属零件打印完成_____，需要清理表面粉末。

❷ 首先向设备加入金属粉末，_____用激光进行逐层扫描。

❸ 首先打开"调试"对话框，_____调试缸体和铺粉系统。

❹ 结束_____，升降台上升一层高度。

语法点 2　Grammar Point 2

动词"便于"　The verb "便于"

It indicates making it easy to do something.

1. 把工作缸体底板上升到基准面，便于安装基板。
2. 把材料加热到液体状态，便于凝固形成实物。
3. 把升降台下降一层高度，便于进行第二层扫描。

选词填空。Choose the words to fill in the blanks.

A. 便于　　B. 于　　C. 在

1. 把工作缸体底板上升到基准面以上，_____安装基板。
2. 水冷机控制温度一般_____30 ℃左右。
3. 把材料加热到液体状态，_____凝固形成实物。
4. 检查气压是否大_____2 MPa。

第 20 课 | 操作设备

 汉字书写 Writing Chinese Characters

 职业拓展 Career Insight

A 3D printer can be used in a simple and convenient way. As long as we have mastered how to use the relevant software and settings, we can easily print a variety of practical 3D objects. The technology not only provides strong support for scientific research, industrial design and other fields, but is widely used in our daily life.

193

 **小结 Summary**

1. 听句子选词填空。Listen to the sentences and choose the words to fill in the blanks. 🎧 20-03

| A. 存储器 | B. 功能 | C. 按钮 | D. 便于 |

❶ 将工作缸体底板上升到基准面以上＿＿＿＿安装基板。

❷ 通过＿＿＿＿或网络将模型文件导入计算机。

❸ 根据需要打开加热＿＿＿＿。

❹ 点击＿＿＿＿前后移动铺粉系统，观察是否正常。

2. 看词语练拼音。Look at the words and practice Pinyin.

shǒuxiān	gāngtǐ	duìhuàkuàng	jīzhǔnmiàn
首先	缸体	对话框	基准面
hé	dǐbǎn	shìfǒu	shàngshēng
和	底板	是否	上升

3. 朗读下列句子。Read aloud the following sentences.

❶ Shǒuxiān jiāng yùchǔlǐ de móxíng wénjiàn kǎobèi dào shèbèi de kòngzhì jìsuànjī shang.
首先 将 预处理 的 模型 文件 拷贝 到 设备 的 控制 计算机 上。

❷ Dǎkāi "tiáoshì" duìhuàkuàng, xiān tiáoshì gāngtǐ hé pūfěn xìtǒng.
打开 "调试" 对话框，先 调试 缸体 和 铺粉 系统。

第21课 添加支撑
Lesson 21 Adding Supports

 复习 Revision

1. 根据图片选择词语。Choose the words based on the pictures.

❶ 材料（   ）　　❷ 按钮（   ）　　❸ 计算机（   ）
　 缸体（   ）　　　 技术（   ）　　　 数字（   ）

2. 把下列词语组合成短语或句子。Connect the words into phrases or sentences.

1 ①调试　②打开　③对话框

_____

2 ①按钮　②移动　③点击　④前后

_____

3 ①加热　　②打开　　③功能

_____

 **热身 Warm-up**

你认识这些词语吗？　Do you know these words?

	suōfàng 缩放	scale, zoom
	zhèngquè 正确	correct
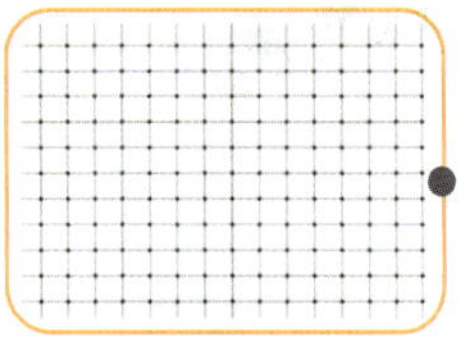	wǎnggé 网格	grid
	xuánkōng 悬空	suspend
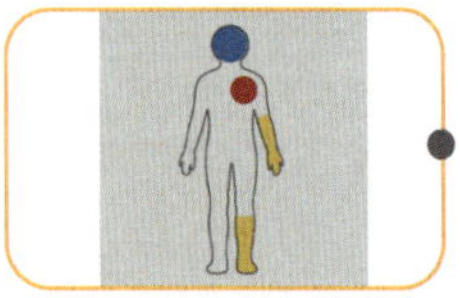	bùwèi 部位	part, section
	shàng 上	indicating the surface of sth.

第 21 课 | 添加支撑

 **学习生词** Words and Expressions 🎧 21-01

1	旋转	xuánzhuǎn	v.	rotate
2	缩放	suōfàng	v.	scale, zoom
3	确保	quèbǎo	v.	ensure
4	正确	zhèngquè	adj.	correct
5	底面	dǐmiàn	n.	base, bottom surface
6	网格	wǎnggé	n.	grid
7	上	shang	n.	*indicating the surface of sth.*
8	适应	shìyìng	v.	fit, adapt
9	调节	tiáojié	v.	adjust
10	悬空	xuánkōng	v.	suspend
11	部位	bùwèi	n.	part, section
12	范围	fànwéi	n.	range, scope
13	结构	jiégòu	n.	structure
14	务必	wùbì	adv.	must, be sure to
15	转换	zhuǎnhuàn	v.	convert

词语练习 Word Exercises

1. 学习词语搭配。Study the collocations.

❶ zhèngquè 正确	wèizhì zhèngquè 位置 正确	the position is correct
	géshi zhèngquè 格式 正确	the format is correct
❷ shìyìng 适应	shìyìng huánjìng 适应 环境	adapt to the environment
	shìyìng jīqì 适应 机器	adapt to the machine
❸ zhuǎnhuàn 转换	zhuǎnhuàn géshi 转换 格式	convert the format
	zhuǎnhuàn wénjiàn 转换 文件	convert the file

2. 给词语选择正确搭配。Choose the right words to form collocations.

❶ suōfàng
　缩放_____　　A. zuòbiāo 坐标　　B. jīqì 机器

❷ shìyìng
　适应_____　　A. gōngzuò 工作　　B. xìnxī 信息

❸ xuánkōng
　悬空_____　　A. gōngjù 工具　　B. bùwèi 部位

学习课文 Text 🎧 21-02

第一步：导入绘制完成的模型文件。

第二步：使用移动、旋转和缩放工具对模型进行调整，确保模型的位置正确，模型的底面在网格上。

第三步：把模型调整到适应打印机的打印尺寸。

第四步：调节悬空部位添加支撑的范围大小等支撑结构参数。

第五步：添加完成支撑后，务必将文件的格式转换为STL格式。

Step 1: Import the model file that has been drawn.

Step 2: Use Move, Rotate, and Scale tools to adjust the model, ensuring that the position of the model is correct and the bottom of the model is on the grid.

Step 3: Adjust the model to fit the printing size of the printer.

Step 4: Adjust the range, size, and other support structure parameters for adding support to the suspended part.

Step 5: After adding the support, be sure to convert the file to the STL format.

课文练习 Text Exercises

1. 回答问题。Answer the questions.

① 需要使用坐标工具对模型进行调整吗?

② 不用调整模型以适应打印机的打印尺寸吗?

2. 根据课文选词填空。Choose the words to fill in the blanks based on the text.

A. 范围　　　B. 缩放　　　C. 确保　　　D. 到

① _____ 模型的位置正确。

② 把模型调整 _____ 适应打印机的打印尺寸。

第 21 课｜添加支撑

 学习语法 Grammar

 语法点 1 Grammar Point 1

动词"确保"　The verb "确保"

It means "to ensure" and is usually followed by a verb or an adjective.

1. 确保模型的位置正确。
2. 确保模型的底面在网格上。
3. 确保在相应位置添加支撑。

把下列词语组合成短语或句子。Connect the words into phrases or sentences.

1. 请　STL 格式　文件　是　确保　格式

_____

2. 模型　怎么　确保　不　变形

_____

3. 请　厚度　相等　确保　分层　的　是　的

_____

4. 确保　在　支撑　位置　相应　添加

_____

201

语法点 2 Grammar Point 2

副词"务必" The adverb "务必"

It is used before a verb to indicate "must, be sure to".

1. 文件格式务必转换为 STL 格式。
2. 模型打印前务必添加支撑。
3. 对模型进行软件切片的时候,务必进行检查。

给"务必"选择正确的位置。Choose the right positions for "务必".

1. A 大家 B 按时上班、下班 C。 (　　)
2. A 模型打印前 B 进行预处理 C。 (　　)
3. A 将文件格式保存 B 为 STL 格式 C。 (　　)
4. A 设定 B 好重要的 C 打印参数。 (　　)

汉字书写 Writing Chinese Characters

dà
大

yìng
应

第 21 课 | 添加支撑

 文化拓展 Culture Insight

The Palace Museum in Beijing, formerly known as the Forbidden City, served as the royal palace for the Ming (1368–1644) and Qing (1644–1911) dynasties in China and is situated at the heart of Beijing's central axis. The structures within the Palace Museum are divided into the Outer Court and the Inner Court. The center of the Outer Court houses the Hall of Supreme Harmony, the Hall of Central Harmony, and the Hall of Preserving Harmony, collectively known as the Three Great Halls, which were used for grand national ceremonies in ancient times. The Palace Museum spans an area of approximately 720,000 square meters, with a floor area of about 150,000 square meters. Additionally, it includes over 70 palaces of varying sizes and 8,707 rooms, as measured by experts on-site in 1973.

 小结 Summary

1. 听句子选词填空。Listen to the sentences and choose the words to fill in the blanks. 🎧 21-03

> A. 适应　　B. 范围　　C. 底面　　D. 转换

❶ 确保模型的位置正确，模型的_____在网格上。

❷ 调节悬空部位添加支撑_____的大小。

❸ 把支撑_____为实体，并导出 STL 格式的文件。

❹ 把模型调整到_____打印机的打印尺寸。

2. 看词语练拼音。Look at the words and practice Pinyin.

dàxiǎo	zuòbiāo	tiānjiā	quèbǎo
大小	坐标	添加	确保
tiáozhěng	xuánkōng	dào	suōfàng
调整	悬空	到	缩放

3. 朗读下列句子。Read aloud the following sentences.

❶ Dǎorù huìzhì wánchéng de móxíng wénjiàn.
导入 绘制 完成 的 模型 文件。

❷ Shǐyòng yídòng、xuánzhuǎn hé suōfàng gōngjù duì móxíng jìnxíng tiáozhěng.
使用 移动、旋转 和 缩放 工具 对 模型 进行 调整。

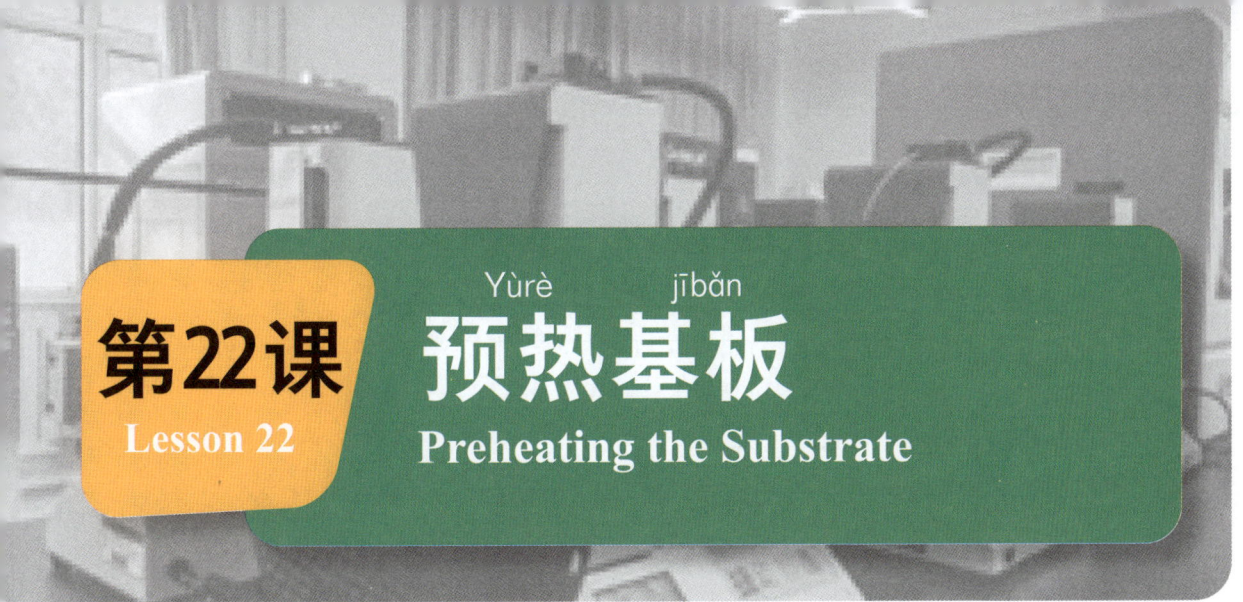

第22课 Lesson 22

预热基板 Yùrè jībǎn
Preheating the Substrate

 复习 Revision

1. 根据图片选择词语。Choose the words based on the pictures.

  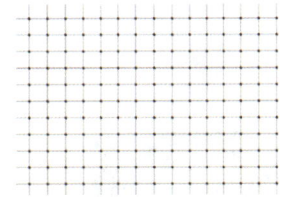

❶ 正确（　　）　　❷ 按下（　　）　　❸ 网格（　　）
　 正常（　　）　　　 上（　　）　　　 网络（　　）

2. 把下列词语组合成短语或句子。Connect the words into phrases or sentences.

❶ ①坐标　②使用　③工具　④缩放

_____

❷ ①文件　②绘制完成的　③导入　④模型

_____

3 ①确保　②位置　③正确　④模型

___

 热身 Warm-up

你认识这些词语吗？ Do you know these words?

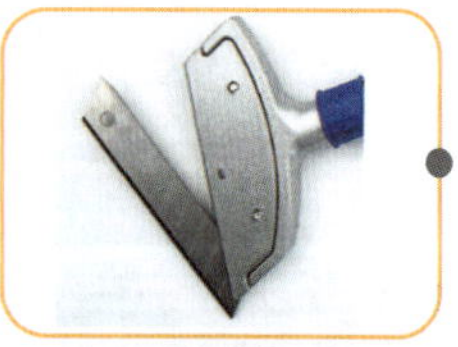

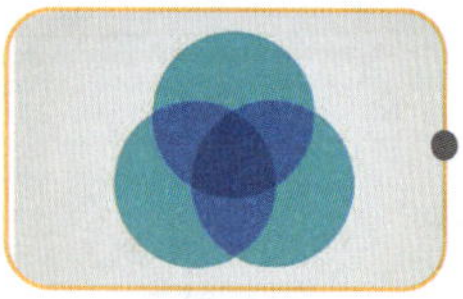

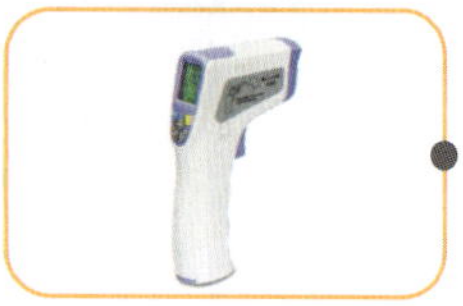

	sāichǐ 塞尺	feeler gauge
	guādāo 刮刀	scraper
	máocì 毛刺	burr
	bōwén 波纹	ripple
	chóngdié 重叠	overlap
	cèwēnyí 测温仪	thermometer

第 22 课 | 预热基板

 学习生词 Words and Expressions  22-01

1	符合	fúhé	*v.*	conform to
2	要求	yāoqiú	*n.*	requirement
3	塞尺	sāichǐ	*n.*	feeler gauge
4	刮刀	guādāo	*n.*	scraper
5	区域	qūyù	*n.*	area
6	摩擦力	mócālì	*n.*	friction
7	相同	xiāngtóng	*adj.*	same
8	一致	yīzhì	*adj.*	consistent
9	间隙	jiànxì	*n.*	gap
10	没有	méiyǒu	*v.*	not have
11	毛刺	máocì	*n.*	burr
12	波纹	bōwén	*n.*	ripple
13	重叠	chóngdié	*n.*	overlap
14	等待	děngdài	*v.*	wait
15	测温仪	cèwēnyí	*n.*	thermometer

📖 **词语练习 Word Exercises**

1. 学习词语搭配。Study the collocations.

❶ fúhé 符合	fúhé yāoqiú 符合 要求	meet the requirements
	fúhé tiáojiàn 符合 条件	meet the conditions
❷ chóngdié 重叠	chóngdié bùfen 重叠 部分	overlapping part
	chóngdié qūyù 重叠 区域	overlapping area
❸ yāoqiú 要求	hélǐ yāoqiú 合理 要求	reasonable requirement
	fúhé yāoqiú 符合 要求	meet the requirements

2. 给词语选择正确搭配。Choose the right words to form collocations.

❶ xiāngtóng 相同_____   A. qíngkuàng 情况   B. fúhé 符合

❷ dǎkāi 打开_____   A. ruǎnjiàn 软件   B. duì de 对 的

❸ yāoqiú 要求_____   A. xuǎnzé 选择   B. yízhì 一致

学习课文 Text 🎧 22-02

第一步：确保基板符合要求。

第二步：把基板安装到底板上。

第三步：塞尺在基板和刮刀之间的区域摩擦力相同，确保它们有一致的间隙。

第四步：观察铺粉是否铺平，还应该确保没有毛刺、波纹、重叠等情况。

第五步：设置加热温度，等待基板加热，使用测温仪测量温度，确保基板温度正确。

Step 1: Ensure that the substrate meets the requirements.

Step 2: Install the substrate onto the base plate.

Step 3: The friction of the feeler gauge in the area between the substrate and the scraper is the same. Ensure that they have a consistent gap.

Step 4: Observe whether the powder is evenly spread and ensure that there are no burrs, ripples, overlaps, etc.

Step 5: Set the heating temperature, and wait for the substrate to heat up. Use a thermometer to measure the temperature, and ensure that the substrate temperature is correct.

课文练习 Text Exercises

1. 回答问题。Answer the questions.

① 是否将基板安装到底板上？

② 基板和刮刀之间的间隙不需要一致吗？

2. 根据课文选词填空。Choose the words to fill in the blanks based on the text.

A. 测温仪	B. 间隙	C. 等待	D. 波纹

① 观察铺粉是否铺平，还应确保没有毛刺、_____等情况。

② 打开操作软件的基板加热功能，设置加热仪温度，然后_____基板加热。

学习语法 Grammar

 语法点 1　Grammar Point 1

方位词"之间"　The word of location "之间"

It indicates between two places, time periods, people, things, or quantities.

1. 塞尺在基板和刮刀之间的区域摩擦力相同。
2. 它们之间的间隙相同吗？
3. 层和层之间的厚度是相等的。

给"之间"选择正确的位置。Choose the right positions for "之间".

1. A 塞尺在基板和刮刀 B 的区域的摩擦力 C 相同。
2. A 它们 B 的间隙 C 相同吗？
3. A 层 B 和层 C 的厚度是相等的。
4. A 水冷机控制温度一般 B 在 21 ℃ 到 30 ℃ C。

语法点 2 Grammar Point 2

能愿动词"应该" The optative verb "应该"

　　It is used before a verb or an adjective to indicate that something should be done.

❶ 应该确保没有毛刺、波纹、重叠等情况。

❷ 你应该先打开软件。

❸ 模型文件格式应该转换为 STL 格式。

给"应该"选择正确的位置。Choose the right positions for "应该".

❶ A 你 B 选择 C "创建文件"。

❷ A 打印模型前，B 准备好 C 打印材料。

❸ A 把 B 热塑性材料 C 加热到液体状态。

❹ A 确保 B 没有 C 毛刺、波纹、重叠等情况。

 汉字书写 Writing Chinese Characters

职业拓展 Career Insight

Before operating the 3D printer, it is necessary to start the rapid photocuring device in advance to allow the temperature of the resin material to reach the preset reasonable level. After the laser is ignited, additional time is required for it to stabilize. Once the device is running normally, launch the manufacturing control software and load the layered data file generated during preprocessing.

小结 Summary

1. 听句子选词填空。Listen to the sentences and choose the words to fill in the blanks. 🎧 22-03

> A. 测温仪　　B. 较大　　C. 摩擦力　　D. 毛刺

① 将铺粉盒移动到后端，观察铺的粉是否有_____、重叠等情况，如果有，则需调整基板平面。

② 需使塞尺在整个基板和刮刀之间的区域内的_____都是大致相同的。

③ 塞尺在刮刀下左右移动有_____摩擦力。

④ 打开操作软件的基板加热功能，设置加热仪温度，然后等待基板加热，用红外_____测量温度，在预热的同时可以进行下一步添加粉末。

2. 看词语练拼音。Look at the words and practice Pinyin.

děngdài	fúhé	máocì	tuīyí
等待	符合	毛刺	推移
chóngdié	bōwén	jiànxì	sāichǐ
重叠	波纹	间隙	塞尺

3. 朗读下列句子。Read aloud the following sentences.

① Jiāng jībǎn ānzhuāng dào gōngzuò gāngtǐ dǐbǎn shang.
　将 基板 安装 到 工作 缸体 底板 上。

② Shèzhì jiārè wēndù, děngdài jībǎn biànrè.
　设置 加热 温度，等待 基板 变热。

第23课 操作激光器
Lesson 23 Operating Lasers

 复习 Revision

1. 根据图片选择词语。Choose the words based on the pictures.

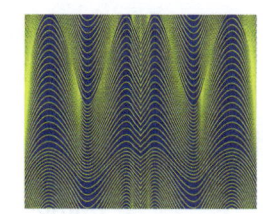 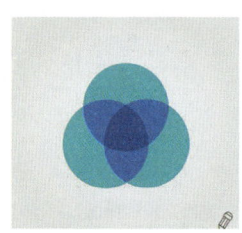 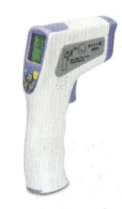

❶ 波纹（   ）　　❷ 重叠（   ）　　❸ 刮刀（   ）
　 间隙（   ）　　　 区域（   ）　　　 测温仪（   ）

2. 把下列词语组合成短语或句子。Connect the words into phrases or sentences.

❶ ①要求　　②确保　　③基板　　④符合

　 _____

❷ ①上　　②安装　　③底板　　④到

　 _____

3 ①测温仪　　②温度　　③使用　　④测量

_____

热身 Warm-up

你认识这些词语吗？ Do you know these words?

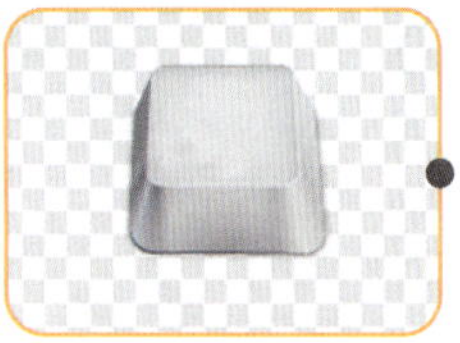	ànjiàn 按键	button
	duànkāi 断开	disconnect
	shùzhí 数值	numerical value
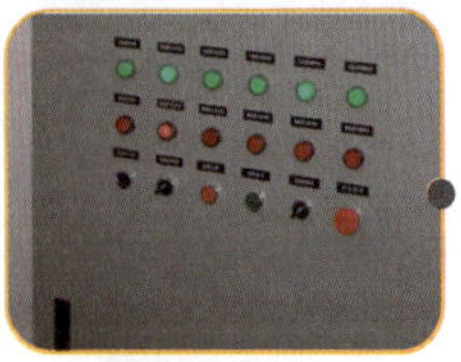	kòngzhìguì 控制柜	control cabinet
	jiàngdī 降低	reduce
	miànbǎn 面板	panel

学习生词 Words and Expressions  23-01

1	按键	ànjiàn	n.	button
2	控制柜	kòngzhìguì	n.	control cabinet
3	里面	lǐmiàn	n.	within, inside
4	分钟	fēnzhōng	n.	minute
5	面板	miànbǎn	n.	panel
6	显示	xiǎnshì	v.	display
7	完全	wánquán	adv.	completely
8	稳定	wěndìng	adj.	steady, stable
9	加载	jiāzài	v.	upload, load
10	电流	diànliú	n.	electrical current
11	数值	shùzhí	n.	numerical value
12	必须	bìxū	adv.	must
13	断开	duànkāi	phr.	disconnect
14	降低	jiàngdī	v.	reduce
15	控制器	kòngzhìqì	n.	controller

词语练习 Word Exercises

1. 学习词语搭配。Study the collocations.

❶ duànkāi 断开	duànkāi liánjiē 断开 连接	disconnect
	duànkāi kāiguān 断开 开关	turn off the switch
❷ jiàngdī 降低	jiàngdī shēngyīn 降低 声音	lower the volume
	jiàngdī shùzhí 降低 数值	reduce the numerical value
❸ jiāzài 加载	jiāzài diànliú 加载 电流	load the current
	jiāzài zhòngliàng 加载 重量	load the weight

2. 给词语选择正确搭配。Choose the right words to form collocations.

❶ wánquán 完全 _____ A. wěndìng 稳定   B. miànbǎn 面板

❷ diànliú 电流 _____ A. lǐmiàn 里面   B. liánjiē 连接

❸ xiǎnshì 显示 _____ A. zhèngcháng 正常   B. děngdài 等待

学习课文 Text 🎧 23-02

第一步：按下控制按键，激光系统通电。

第二步：打开控制柜里面的电源开关，10分钟后，观察面板界面是否显示正常。

第三步：等待温度完全稳定后，加载电流到设定数值。

第四步：关闭激光器的时候，必须先断开电流连接。

第五步：电流数值降低到0的时候，再把控制器的电源开关关闭。

Step 1: Press the control button to power up the laser system.

Step 2: Turn on the power switch in the control cabinet. After 10 minutes, observe whether the panel interface displays normally.

Step 3: Wait for the temperature to stabilize completely, and then load the current to the set value.

Step 4: Before turning off the laser, you must disconnect the current connection first.

Step 5: When the current value drops to 0, turn off the power switch of the controller.

课文练习 Text Exercises

1. 回答问题。Answer the questions.

    ① 你会打开电源开关吗？

    ② 你会加载电流到设定数值吗？

2. 根据课文选词填空。Choose the words to fill in the blanks based on the text.

    A. 打开   B. 关闭   C. 按下   D. 设定

    ① _____ 控制柜里面的电源开关。

    ② 加载电流到_____数值。

 学习语法 Grammar

 语法点 1 Grammar Point 1

动词 + 下　Verb + 下

"下" is used after a verb to indicate the downward direction of an action.

1. 按下开关。

2. 按下控制按键。

3. 请放下工具。

选词填空。Choose the words to fill in the blanks.

A. 下　　　B. 好

1. 按_____按钮。

2. 参数设定_____了吗?

3. 按_____开关。

4. 请准备_____打印材料。

语法点 2　Grammar Point 2

> 等（待）……后，……　wait until..., (do)...
>
> It indicates that the subsequent operation can be started only after certain conditions are met.

1. 等待温度稳定后，加载电流到设定值。
2. 等设定好参数后，再开始打印模型。
3. 等工作缸底板上升到基准面后，我们再安装基板。

选词填空。Choose the words to fill in the blanks.

A. 等待　　　　B. 等

1. _____温度稳定后，加载电流到设定值。
2. _____设定好参数后，再开始打印模型。
3. 检查是否遗落螺钉、工具、毛刷_____物品。
4. 我们需要进行打磨、抛光、喷绘_____处理。

汉字书写　Writing Chinese Characters

xiǎn

显 显 显 显 显 显 显 显 显

第 23 课 | 操作激光器

 文化拓展 Culture Insight

Chopsticks are a symbol of Chinese culinary culture and among the most commonly used eating utensils worldwide. They originated in China, with ivory chopsticks appearing over 3,000 years ago. Later, they were introduced to other Asian regions such as Korea, Japan, and Vietnam. Chopsticks are typically made from materials such as bamboo, wood, bone, porcelain, metal, and plastic. Serving chopsticks also originated in China, where both shared meals and the use of serving chopsticks have long-standing cultural roots.

小结 Summary

1. 听句子选词填空。 Listen to the sentences and choose the words to fill in the blanks. 🎧 23-03

| A. 打开 | B. 关闭 | C. 按下 | D. 设定 |

❶ _____ 控制柜里面的电源开关。

❷ 加载电流到_____数值。

❸ _____控制按键。

❹ _____激光器的时候，必须先断开电流连接。

2. 看词语练拼音。 Look at the words and practice Pinyin.

ànjiàn　　　　　lǐmiàn　　　　　miànbǎn　　　　jiàngdī
按键　　　　　　里面　　　　　　面板　　　　　　降低

shùzhí　　　　　xiǎnshì　　　　　fēnzhōng　　　　wěndìng
数值　　　　　　显示　　　　　　分钟　　　　　　稳定

3. 朗读下列句子。 Read aloud the following sentences.

❶ Děngdài wēndù wánquán wěndìng hòu, jiāzài diànliú dào shèdìng shùzhí.
等待 温度 完全 稳定 后，加载 电流 到 设定 数值。

❷ Diànliú shùzhí jiàngdī dào 0 de shíhou, zài bǎ kòngzhìqì de diànyuán kāiguān guānbì.
电流 数值 降低 到 0 的 时候，再 把 控制器 的 电源 开关 关闭。

第24课 Lesson 24
Cèshì guānglù
测试光路
Testing the Optical Path

 复习 Revision

1. 根据图片选择词语。 Choose the words based on the pictures.

❶ 降低（　　）　　❷ 断开（　　）　　❸ 电流（　　）
　 加载（　　）　　　 连接（　　）　　　 数值（　　）

2. 把下列词语组合成短语或句子。 Connect the words into phrases or sentences.

1️⃣　①打开　　②开关　　③电源

_____

2️⃣　①控制　　②按下　　③按键

_____

225

3 ①稳定 ②等待 ③后 ④温度

_____

 热身 Warm-up

你认识这些词语吗？ Do you know these words?

- zhǐ 纸 — paper
- kǎchǐ 卡尺 — caliper
- jiāo 胶 — glue, adhesive
- chángdù 长度 — length
- fāngkuài 方块 — square
- biānkuàng 边框 — frame

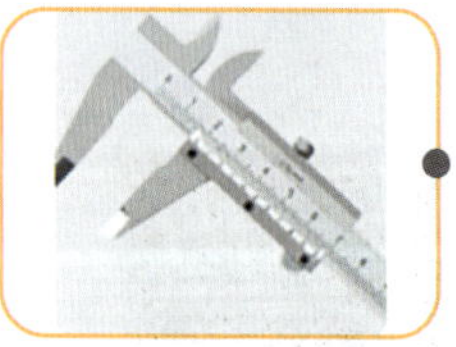

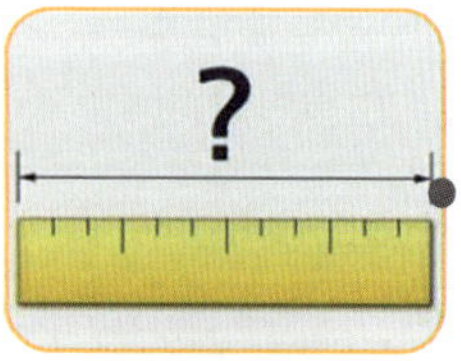

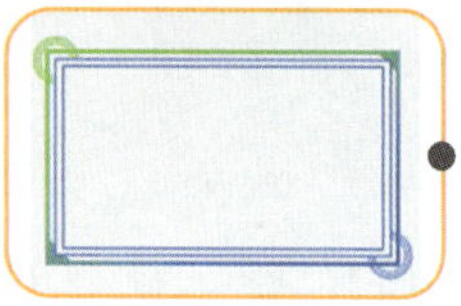

第 24 课 | 测试光路

学习生词 Words and Expressions 24-01

1	激光头	jīguāngtóu	*n.*	laser head
2	测光	cèguāng	*v.*	measure the light
3	专用	zhuānyòng	*v.*	used for a special purpose
4	薄	báo	*adj.*	thin
5	双面胶	shuāngmiànjiāo	*n.*	double-sided tape
	双面	shuāngmiàn	*phr.*	double-sided
6	粘贴	zhāntiē	*v.*	paste, adhere
7	纸	zhǐ	*n.*	paper
8	方块	fāngkuài	*n.*	square
9	象限	xiàngxiàn	*n.*	quadrant
10	前门	qiánmén	*n.*	front door
11	卡尺	kǎchǐ	*n.*	caliper
12	边长	biāncháng	*n.*	side length
13	边框	biānkuàng	*n.*	frame
14	长度	chángdù	*n.*	length

227

词语练习 Word Exercises

1. 学习词语搭配。Study the collocations.

shuāngmiàn ① 双面	shuāngmiàn dǎyìn 双面 打印	double-sided printing
	shuāngmiàn bōli 双面 玻璃	double-sided glass
zhāntiē ② 粘贴	zhāntiē miànbǎn 粘贴 面板	paste the panel
	fùzhì zhāntiē 复制 粘贴	copy and paste
zhuānyòng ③ 专用	zhuānyòng shèbèi 专用 设备	specialized equipment
	zhuānyòng jībǎn 专用 基板	dedicated substrate

2. 给词语选择正确搭配。Choose the right words to form collocations.

① _____ jībǎn 基板　　A. zhuānyòng 专用　　B. shuāngmiàn 双面

② cèliáng 测量 _____　　A. biāncháng 边长　　B. xiàngxiàn 象限

③ _____ gōngnéng 功能　　A. jiārè 加热　　B. cèguāng 测光

学习课文 Text 🎧 24-02

第一步：检查激光头是否移动或脱落，指示灯是否正常。

第二步：安装测光专用基板，用薄双面胶粘贴测光纸。

第三步：打开加热功能，观察底板是否已经加热。

第四步：观察激光是否扫描出方块和象限，关闭激光电源，打开前门并用卡尺测量方块边长和边框长度，看长度是否一致。

Step 1:　Check whether the laser head has moved or detached, and whether the indicator light is normal.

Step 2:　Install the dedicated substrate for light measurement, and adhere the light-measuring paper using thin double-sided tape.

Step 3:　Start the heating function and observe whether the base plate has been heated.

Step 4:　Observe whether the laser scans out squares and quadrants. Turn off the laser power, open the front door, and use a caliper to measure whether the side lengths of the squares and the lengths of the frames are consistent.

课文练习 Text Exercises

1. 回答问题。Answer the questions.

① 你会安装测光机专用基板吗?

② 你会用双面胶粘贴测光纸吗?

2. 根据课文选词填空。Choose the words to fill in the blanks based on the text.

> A. 检查　　B. 关闭　　C. 打开　　D. 观察

① _____ 激光是否扫描出方块和象限。

② _____ 激光头是否移动或脱落。

第 24 课 | 测试光路

学习语法 Grammar

 语法点 1　Grammar Point 1

副词"已经"　The adverb "已经"

　　It is used before a verb to indicate that an action or a change has already been completed or reached a certain degree.

1. 观察底板是否已经加热。
2. 模型已经打印好了。
3. 请确保已经打开激光器。

连词成句。Connect the words into sentences.

1. 是否　观察　已经　底板　加热

    _____

2. 创建　我　了　已经　文件

    _____

3. 指示灯　电源　亮起　已经

    _____

4. 3D　已经　打印　领域　可以　工业　用　在　了

    _____

231

语法点 2 Grammar Point 2

动词 + 出（来） Verb + 出（来）

"出(来)" is used after a verb to indicate that an action has caused something to start from scratch or to emerge.

1. 观察激光是否扫描出方块和象限。
2. 请大声说出你的名字。
3. 他从包里拿出了一张纸。

选词填空。Choose the words to fill in the blanks.

| A. 下 | B. 出 |

1. 观察激光是否扫描_____方块和象限。
2. 请大声说_____你的名字。
3. 按_____电源开关。
4. 按_____控制按钮。

汉字书写 Writing Chinese Characters

第 24 课 | 测试光路

| fāng |
| 方 |

| shuāng |
| 双 |

| guò |
| 过 |

职业拓展 Career Insight

When heat treatment is performed during postprocessing, the selection of high heating frequency is based on the requirements of heat treatment and heating depth. The higher the frequency is, the shallower the heating depth will be. The heating depth of the high frequency (above 10 kHz) is 0.5–2.5 mm, which is usually used for heating small and medium-sized parts, such as small module gears and small and medium-sized shaft parts.

 小结 Summary

1. 听句子选词填空。Listen to the sentences and choose the words to fill in the blanks. 🎧 24-03

> A. 检查　　　B. 关闭　　　C. 打开　　　D. 观察

❶ _____激光是否扫描出方块和象限。

❷ _____激光头是否移动或脱落。

❸ 你会_____加热功能吗?

❹ 你_____激光电源了吗?

2. 看词语练拼音。Look at the words and practice Pinyin.

cèguāng	zhuānyòng	shuāngmiàn	kǎchǐ
测光	专用	双面	卡尺
biāncháng	jīguāngtóu	biānkuàng	chángdù
边长	激光头	边框	长度

3. 朗读下列句子。Read aloud the following sentences.

❶ 检查 激光头 是否 移动 或 脱落,指示灯 是否 正常。
Jiǎnchá jīguāngtóu shìfǒu yídòng huò tuōluò, zhǐshìdēng shìfǒu zhèngcháng.

❷ 打开 加热 功能,观察 底板 是否 已经 加热。
Dǎkāi jiārè gōngnéng, guānchá dǐbǎn shìfǒu yǐjīng jiārè.

第25课 Lesson 25
设置参数 Shèzhì cānshù
Setting Parameters

 复习 Revision

1. 根据图片选择词语。Choose the words based on the pictures.

 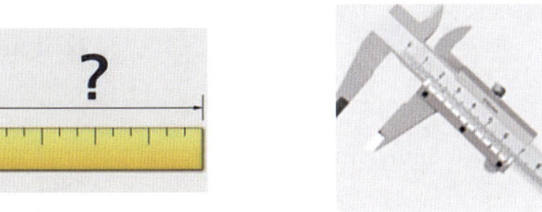 

❶ 长度（   ）　　❷ 卡尺（   ）　　❸ 方块（   ）
　 前门（   ）　　　 边长（   ）　　　 边框（   ）

2. 把下列词语组合成短语或句子。Connect the words into phrases or sentences.

❶ ①你会　②吗　③打开　④加热　⑤功能

_____

❷ ①关闭　②电源　③激光

_____

3 ①卡尺   ②边框   ③方块   ④测量   ⑤用   ⑥长度

热身 Warm-up

你认识这些词语吗？ Do you know these words?

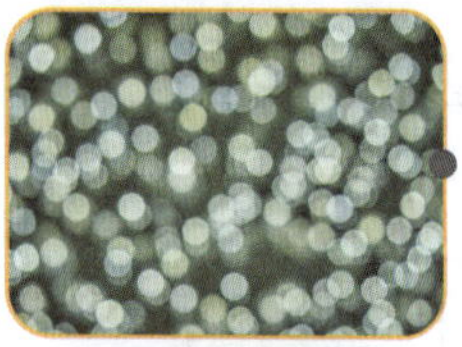

càidān 菜单 — menu

guāngbān 光斑 — light spot

fāngxiàng 方向 — direction

yìngjiàn 硬件 — hardware

xìshù 系数 — coefficient

jiānjù 间距 — spacing

 学习生词 Words and Expressions  25-01

1	菜单	càidān	n.	menu
2	硬件	yìngjiàn	n.	hardware
3	修改	xiūgǎi	v.	modify
4	制作	zhìzuò	v.	produce
5	间距	jiānjù	n.	spacing
6	光斑	guāngbān	n.	light spot
7	补偿	bǔcháng	v.	compensate
8	方向	fāngxiàng	n.	direction
9	修正	xiūzhèng	v.	correct
10	系数	xìshù	n.	coefficient
11	方式	fāngshì	n.	method
12	实际	shíjì	adj.	actual
13	其他	qítā	pron.	other
14	经验	jīngyàn	n.	experience
15	实时	shíshí	adv.	real-time
16	确定	quèdìng	v.	confirm

词语练习 Word Exercises

1. 学习词语搭配。Study the collocations.

❶ zhìzuò 制作	zhìzuò gōngyì 制作 工艺	production process
	zhìzuò chǎnpǐn 制作 产品	make products
❷ fāngxiàng 方向	fāngxiàng zhèngquè 方向 正确	the direction is correct
	fāngxiàng zhǐyǐn 方向 指引	direction guidance
❸ xiūgǎi 修改	xiūgǎi wánshàn 修改 完善	modify and improve
	xiūgǎi bǔchōng 修改 补充	modify and supplement

2. 给词语选择正确搭配。Choose the right words to form collocations.

❶ zhìzuò 制作_____ A. gōngyì 工艺 B. jiānjù 间距

❷ yìngjiàn 硬件_____ A. shèbèi 设备 B. xìshù 系数

❸ xiūgǎi 修改_____ A. wánshàn 完善 B. quèdìng 确定

第25课 | 设置参数

 学习课文 Text 🎧 25-02

第一步：点击设备软件菜单，选择"硬件设置"和"修改工艺"。

第二步：设置制作参数。主要包括扫描速度，激光功率，烧结间距，光斑补偿，层厚，X、Y、Z方向修正系数，扫描方式等。其中，层厚根据实际工艺要求调整，其他根据经验进行实时调整。

第三步：设置完成后，点击"确定"按键，完成参数设置。

Step 1: Click the menu of the device software. Select "Hardware Settings" and "Modify Processing".

Step 2: Set the production parameters, mainly including the scanning speed, laser power, sintering spacing, light spot compensation, layer thickness, correction coefficients in the X, Y, Z directions, scanning method, etc. Among them, adjust the layer thickness according to the actual processing requirements, and adjust the other parameters in real time based on experience.

Step 3: After setting the parameters, click the "OK" button to complete the parameter settings.

课文练习 Text Exercises

1. 回答问题。Answer the questions.

① 你会设置制作参数吗?

② 层厚根据实际工艺要求调整吗?

2. 根据课文选词填空。Choose the words to fill in the blanks based on the text.

A. 制作   B. 修正   C. 补偿   D. 经验

① 设置_____参数。

② 其他根据_____进行实时调整。

学习语法 Grammar

语法点 1　Grammar Point 1

方位词"其中"　The word of location "其中"

It indicates among the persons or things mentioned above.

1. 其中单层厚度根据实际过程实时调整。
2. 操作切片软件需要设定层厚、壁厚和填充密度，其中层厚的意思是切片厚度。
3. 测试光路需要四步，其中第三步是打开加热功能。

选词填空。Choose the words to fill in the blanks.

A. 其中　　　B. 之间

1. _____单层厚度根据实际过程实时调整。
2. 需要设定三个打印参数，_____填充密度已经设定好了。
3. 塞尺在基板和刮刀_____的区域摩擦力相同。
4. 它们_____的间隙相同吗？

语法点 2 Grammar Point 2

代词"其他" The pronoun "其他"

It means "else" or "the rest", indicating the people or things other than those mentioned above.

1. 其他根据经验进行实时调整。
2. 我会打开软件,其他操作不会。
3. 增材制造技术可以用在工业领域,还可以用在其他领域吗?

选词填空。Choose the words to fill in the blanks.

> A. 其他   B. 还

1. 我会说中文,＿＿＿＿人不会。
2. 我会打开软件,＿＿＿＿操作不会。
3. 增材制造技术可以用在工业领域,＿＿＿＿可以用在什么领域?
4. 打印文件的时候,需要转换文件格式,＿＿＿＿需要准备打印材料。

汉字书写 Writing Chinese Characters

shì

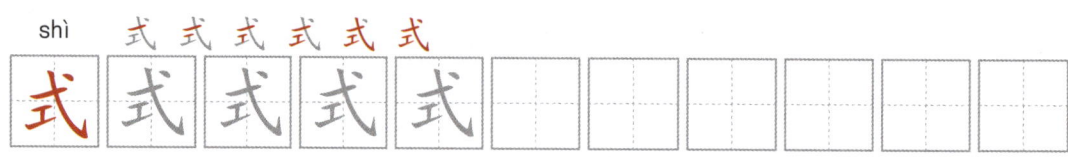

文化拓展 Culture Insight

Online shopping involves searching for product information on the Internet, submitting purchase requests via electronic order forms, and making payments through platforms such as WeChat, Alipay, or online banking. Manufacturers then ship the goods by mail or deliver them to customers' homes through delivery companies. In China, the payment methods for online shopping typically include payment upon delivery (via direct bank transfer or online remittance) and cash on delivery for guaranteed transactions.

 小结 Summary

1. 听句子选词填空。 Listen to the sentences and choose the words to fill in the blanks. 🎧 25-03

> A. 设置　　B. 修正　　C. 修改　　D. 设备

① 点击_____软件菜单。

② 完成参数_____。

③ 方向_____系数。

④ 选择"硬件设置"和"_____工艺"。

2. 看词语练拼音。 Look at the words and practice Pinyin.

zhìzuò	xiūzhèng	xiūgǎi	shèzhì
制作	修正	修改	设置
fāngxiàng	yìngjiàn	shíjì	jīngyàn
方向	硬件	实际	经验

3. 朗读下列句子。 Read aloud the following sentences.

① Shèzhì wánchéng hòu, diǎnjī "quèdìng" ànjiàn, wánchéng cānshù shèzhì.
设置 完成 后，点击"确定"按键，完成 参数 设置。

② Shèzhì zhìzuò cānshù. Zhǔyào bāokuò: sǎomiáo sùdù, jīguāng gōnglǜ, shāojié jiānjù,
设置 制作 参数。主要 包括：扫描 速度，激光 功率，烧结 间距，
guāngbān bǔcháng, cénghòu, X、Y、Z fāngxiàng xiūzhèng xìshù, sǎomiáo fāngshì děng.
光斑 补偿，层厚，X、Y、Z 方向 修正系数，扫描 方式 等。

第26课 Lesson 26
Pànduàn yèwèi 判断液位
Judging Liquid Levels

 复习 Revision

1. 根据图片选择词语。Choose the words based on the pictures.

❶ 间距（　　）　　❷ 方向（　　）　　❸ 菜单（　　）
　实际（　　）　　　方式（　　）　　　系数（　　）

2. 把下列词语组合成短语或句子。Connect the words into phrases or sentences.

❶ ①你会　②设置　③制作　④参数　⑤吗

　_____

❷ ①系数　②方向　③修正　④X、Y、Z

　_____

3 ①软件   ②点击   ③设备   ④菜单

_____

热身 Warm-up

你认识这些词语吗？ Do you know these words?

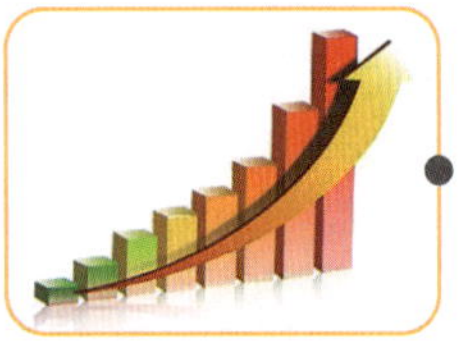	shēnggāo 升高	raise
	tūqǐ 凸起	protrude
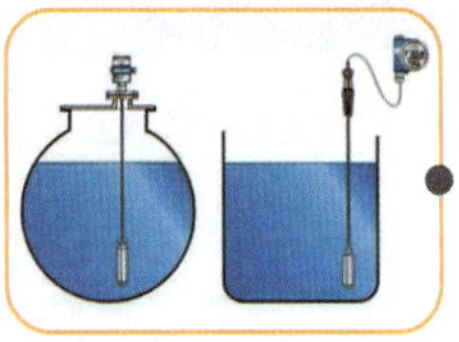	qípíng 齐平	(be) level with
	zhōngjiān 中间	middle
	guādǎo 刮倒	knock over
	gāodù 高度	height

第 26 课 | 判断液位

 **学习生词 Words and Expressions**  26-01

1	当	dāng	*prep.*	(just) at (a time/place), when
2	高度	gāodù	*n.*	height
3	齐平	qípíng	*adj.*	(be) level with
4	液位	yèwèi	*n.*	liquid level
5	合适	héshì	*adj.*	appropriate
6	低于	dīyú	*phr.*	lower than
7	平面	píngmiàn	*n.*	plane
8	中间	zhōngjiān	*n.*	middle
9	凸起	tūqǐ	*v.*	protrude
10	升高	shēnggāo	*phr.*	raise
11	高于	gāoyú	*v.*	higher than
12	降低	jiàngdī	*v.*	lower
13	刮倒	guādǎo	*phr.*	knock over
14	应该	yīnggāi	*opt.*	should
15	距离	jùlí	*n.*	distance

词语练习 Word Exercises

1. 学习词语搭配。Study the collocations.

❶ píngmiàn 平面	píngmiàn shèjì 平面 设计	graphic design
	píngmiàn zhíjiǎo 平面 直角	plane right angle
❷ jiàngdī 降低	jiàngdī fēngxiǎn 降低 风险	reduce the risk
	jiàngdī biāozhǔn 降低 标准	lower the standard
❸ shēnggāo 升高	jiàgé shēnggāo 价格 升高	price rises
	qìwēn shēnggāo 气温 升高	temperature rises

2. 给词语选择正确搭配。Choose the right words to form collocations.

❶ píngmiàn
平面 _____   A. shèjì 设计   B. shēnggāo 升高

❷ jiàngdī
降低 _____   A. fēngxiǎn 风险   B. yèwèi 液位

❸ zhōngjiān
中间 _____   A. wèizhì 位置   B. gāodù 高度

第 26 课 | 判断液位

 **学习课文 Text** 🎧 26-02

第一步: Dì-yī bù: Dāng yètǐ gāodù yǔ guādāo qípíng de shíhou,
当 液体 高度 与 刮刀 齐平 的 时候,
yèwèi héshì.
液位 合适。

第二步: Dì-èr bù: Dāng yètǐ gāodù dīyú guādāo de shíhou, píngmiàn
当 液体 高度 低于 刮刀 的 时候, 平面
zhōngjiān tūqǐ, xūyào shēnggāo yèwèi.
中间 凸起, 需要 升高 液位。

第三步: Dì-sān bù: Dāng yètǐ gāodù gāoyú guādāo dǐmiàn de shíhou,
当 液体 高度 高于 刮刀 底面 的 时候,
xūyào jiàngdī yèwèi.
需要 降低 液位。

第四步: Dì-sì bù: Wèile fángzhǐ língjiàn bèi guādǎo, yèmiàn yīnggāi
为了 防止 零件 被 刮倒, 液面 应该
yǔ guādāo yǒu 0.05 mm de jùlí.
与 刮刀 有 0.05 mm 的 距离。

Step 1: When the liquid height is level with the scraper, the liquid level is appropriate.

Step 2: When the liquid height is lower than the scraper, and the middle of the plane protrudes, you need to raise the liquid level.

Step 3: When the liquid height is higher than the bottom of the scraper, you need to lower the liquid level.

Step 4: To prevent the parts from being knocked over by the scraper, there should be a distance of 0.05 mm between the liquid and the scraper.

课文练习 Text Exercises

1. 回答问题。Answer the questions.

① 你会判断液位是否合适吗？

② 防止零件被刮倒，液面与刮刀之间应该有距离吗？

2. 根据课文选词填空。Choose the words to fill in the blanks based on the text.

| A. 升高 | B. 当 | C. 刮倒 | D. 高度 |

① 平面中间凸起，需要_____液位。

② 防止零件被_____。

第 26 课｜判断液位

 学习语法 Grammar

 语法点 1 Grammar Point 1

介词"与" The preposition "与"

It is used to introduce the other party related to the action. The common structure is: 与 + noun + verbal phrase. It is often used in written Chinese and "跟" is often used in spoken Chinese instead.

1 当液体高度与刮刀齐平的时候，液位合适。

2 液面应该与刮刀有 0.05 mm 的距离。

3 熔融沉积成型与光固化成型不同。

选词填空。Choose the words to fill in the blanks.

A. 与   B. 向

1 当液体高度_____刮刀齐平的时候，液位合适。

2 液面应该_____刮刀有 0.05mm 的距离。

3 _____切片软件导入模型。

4 _____装置注入热塑性材料。

语法点 2 Grammar Point 2

> **"被"字句 "被" sentences**
>
> It is a sentence that indicates that a person or thing has been influenced in some way. The subject is the recipient, and the preposition "被" is used to introduce the agent of the action. The word "被" often implies unpleasant conditions. The common structure is: subject + 被 + object of preposition (agent) + verbal phrase, and the agent following "被" can be omitted. Negative adverbs and modal verbs, if available, should be placed before "被".
>
> ❶ 防止零件被刮倒。
>
> ❷ 材料已经被加热到液体状态了。
>
> ❸ 3D 打印技术被用在工业领域。

选词填空。Choose the words to fill in the blanks.

> A. 被　　　B. 把

❶ 热塑性材料需要_____加热到液体状态。

❷ 需要_____热塑性材料加热到液体状态。

❸ 3D 打印技术_____用在工业领域。

❹ _____3D 打印技术用在工业领域。

汉字书写 Writing Chinese Characters

píng 平
zhǐ 止
hé 合
tū 凸

职业拓展 Career Insight

SLA (Stereolithography Apparatus) technology is primarily used to manufacture various molds and models. Wax molds in investment casting can also be replaced by using SLA prototype molds, obtained? by adding other components to the raw materials. SLA technology offers fast forming speeds and high precision. However, due to resin shrinkage during curing, stress or deformation is inevitable. Therefore, the development trend focuses on creating photosensitive materials with minimal shrinkage, rapid curing, and high strength.

小结 Summary

1. 听句子选词填空。 Listen to the sentences and choose the words to fill in the blanks. 26-03

> A. 升高　　B. 液位　　C. 凸起　　D. 刮倒

1 平面中间_____。

2 需要_____液位。

3 防止零件被_____。

4 你会判断_____是否合适吗？

2. 看词语练拼音。 Look at the words and practice Pinyin.

píngmiàn	tūqǐ	guādǎo	yèwèi
平面	凸起	刮倒	液位
yīnggāi	jùlí	gāoyú	héshì
应该	距离	高于	合适

3. 朗读下列句子。 Read aloud the following sentences.

1 Dāng yètǐ gāodù dīyú guādāo de shíhou, píngmiàn zhōngjiān tūqǐ, xūyào shēnggāo yèwèi.
当液体高度低于刮刀的时候，平面中间凸起，需要升高液位。

2 Dāng yètǐ gāodù gāoyú guādāo dǐmiàn de shíhou, xūyào jiàngdī yèwèi.
当液体高度高于刮刀底面的时候，需要降低液位。

第27课 Lesson 27

校准尺寸 Jiàozhǔn chǐcùn
Calibrating Dimensions

 复习 Revision

1. 根据图片选择词语。Choose the words based on the pictures.

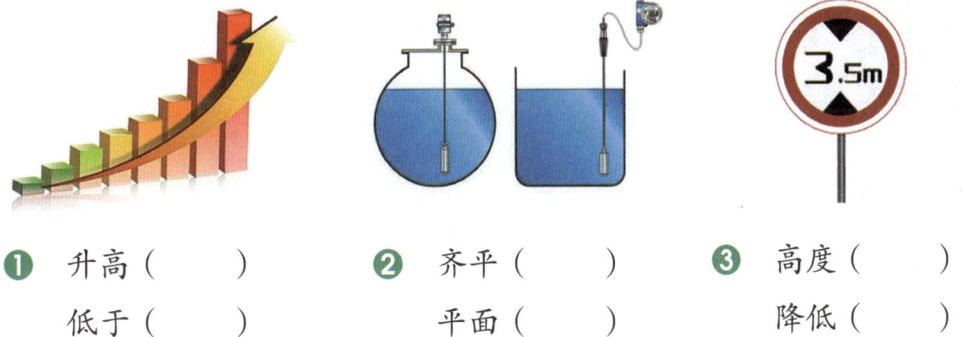

❶ 升高（ ）　　❷ 齐平（ ）　　❸ 高度（ ）
　 低于（ ）　　　 平面（ ）　　　 降低（ ）

2. 把下列词语组合成短语或句子。Connect the words into phrases or sentences.

❶　①防止　②刮倒　③零件　④被

_____

❷　①你会　②合适吗　③液位　④判断　⑤是否

_____

255

3 ①凸起　　②平面　　③中间

_____

 **热身 Warm-up**

你认识这些词语吗？　Do you know these words?

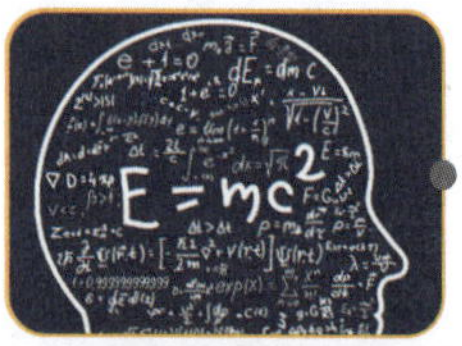	gōngshì 公式	formula
	jiàozhèng 校正	correct
	quèrèn 确认	confirm
	jìsuàn 计算	calculate
	yònglì 用力	apply force
	búyào 不要	(do) not

第27课 | 校准尺寸

 学习生词 Words and Expressions  27-01

1	校准	jiàozhǔn	*v.*	calibrate
2	放平	fàngpíng	*phr.*	lay... flat
3	比较	bǐjiào	*adv.*	relatively
4	薄	báo	*adj.*	thin
5	软	ruǎn	*adj.*	soft
6	不要	búyào	*adv.*	(do) not
7	太	tài	*adv.*	excessively
8	用力	yòng//lì	*v.*	apply force
9	公式	gōngshì	*n.*	formula
10	计算	jìsuàn	*v.*	calculate
11	校正	jiàozhèng	*v.*	correct
12	填入	tiánrù	*phr.*	fill... in
13	相应	xiāngyìng	*v.*	(be) corresponding
14	确认	quèrèn	*v.*	confirm
15	已经	yǐjīng	*adv.*	already

词语练习 Word Exercises

1. 学习词语搭配。Study the collocations.

❶ quèrèn 确认	zàicì quèrèn 再次 确认	reconfirm
	rènzhēn quèrèn 认真 确认	carefully confirm
❷ jiàozhèng 校正	shùjù jiàozhèng 数据 校正	data correction
	zuòbiāo jiàozhèng 坐标 校正	coordinate correction
❸ jìsuàn 计算	kuàisù jìsuàn 快速 计算	quick calculation
	jīngquè jìsuàn 精确 计算	accurate calculation

2. 给词语选择正确搭配。Choose the right words to form collocations.

❶ língjiàn
　零件 _____
　　　　　　　A. fàngpíng 放平　　B. shuǐpíng 水平

❷ jiàozhǔn
　校准 _____
　　　　　　　A. cèliáng 测量　　B. gōngshì 公式

❸ jiàozhèng
　校正 _____
　　　　　　　A. cānshù 参数　　B. fāngxiàng 方向

第27课 ｜ 校准尺寸

 学习课文 Text 🎧 27-02

第一步：Zhìzuò chǐcùn jiàozhǔnjiàn.
制作尺寸校准件。

第二步：Cèliáng X、Y fāngxiàng de chǐcùn, cèliáng de shíhou, bǎ língjiàn fàngpíng, língjiàn bǐjiào báo hé ruǎn de shíhou, búyào tài yònglì.
测量X、Y方向的尺寸，测量的时候，把零件放平，零件比较薄和软的时候，不要太用力。

第三步：Ànzhào jiàozhǔn gōngshì jìsuàn jiàozhèng cānshù.
按照校准公式计算校正参数。

第四步：Bǎ jìsuàn chulai de jiàozhèng cānshù tiánrù xiāngyìng de X jiàozhèng hé Y jiàozhèng de wèizhì, diǎnjī "quèdìng" bǎocún.
把计算出来的校正参数填入相应的X校正和Y校正的位置，点击"确定"保存。

第五步：Chóngxīn dǎkāi ruǎnjiàn, quèrèn chǐcùn yǐjīng xiūgǎi héshì.
重新打开软件，确认尺寸已经修改合适。

Step 1: Make a dimension calibration kit.

Step 2: Measure the dimensions in the X and Y directions. When measuring the dimensions, lay the parts flat. When the parts are relatively thin and soft, do not apply excessive force.

Step 3: Calculate correction parameters according to the calibration formula.

Step 4: Fill the calculated correction parameters in the corresponding X and Y positions for correction, and click "Confirm" to save.

Step 5: Open the software again and confirm that the dimensions have already been modified appropriately.

课文练习 Text Exercises

1. 回答问题。Answer the questions.

① 测量 X、Y 方向的尺寸，测量的时候，需要把零件放平吗？

② 需要按照校准公式计算校正参数吗？

2. 根据课文选词填空。Choose the words to fill in the blanks based on the text.

A. 校正   B. 校准   C. 参数   D. 尺寸

① 你会制作_____校准件吗？

② 重新打开软件，确认_____修改合适。

第27课 | 校准尺寸

 学习语法 Grammar

 语法点 1　Grammar Point 1

副词"比较"　The adverb "比较"

"比较 + adjective" indicates a degree between "slightly" and "very".

1. 金属零件比较薄。
2. 非金属零件比较软。
3. 水冷机控制温度比较高。

把下列词语组合成短语或句子。Connect the words into phrases or sentences.

1. 高度　液体　高　比较

_____

2. 薄　零件　比较　金属

_____

3. 零件　比较　金属　非　软

_____

4. 数值　电流　低　比较

_____

语法点2　Grammar Point 2

副词"太"　The adverb "太"

"太+ adjective (+了)" indicates a degree that is extreme and exceeds the average level. The common negative form is: 不太 + adjective.

1. 不要太用力。
2. 设定好打印参数太重要了。
3. 液面与刮刀的距离太小了。

把下列词语组合成短语或句子。Connect the words into phrases or sentences.

1. 不　粉末　干燥　太

   _____

2. 太　了　均匀　粉末

   _____

3. 非　零件　太　金属　软

   _____

4. 高度　液体　太　高　了

   _____

第 27 课 | 校准尺寸

 **汉字书写** Writing Chinese Characters

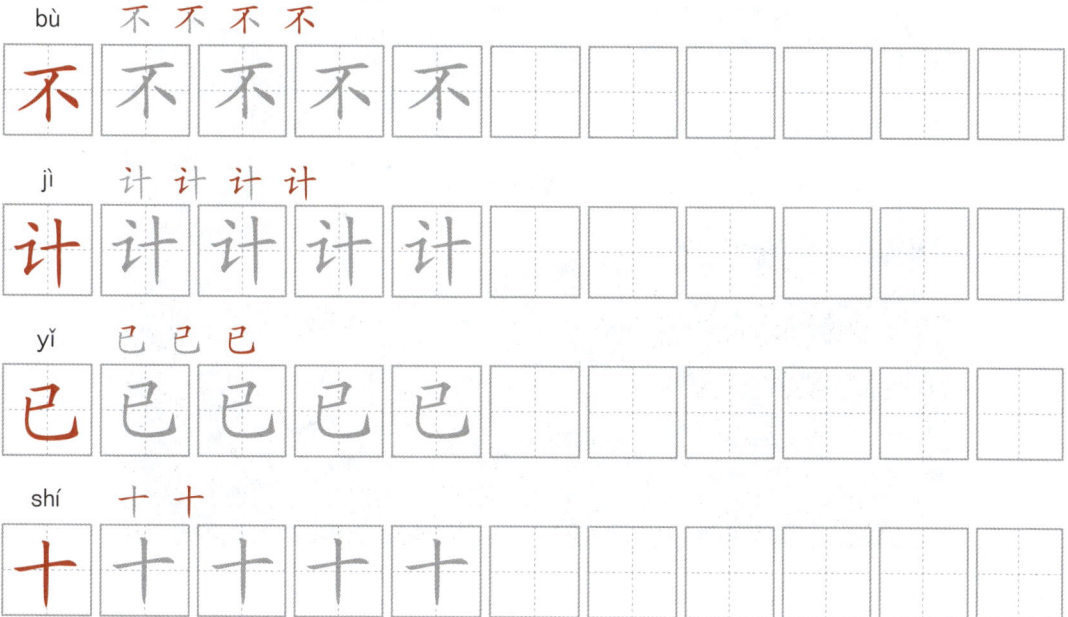

 **文化拓展** Culture Insight

The National Stadium, also known as the "Bird's Nest", was the main stadium for the 2008 Beijing Summer Olympics. It also witnessed the opening and closing ceremonies of the 2008 Beijing Summer Olympics and the 2008 Beijing Paralympic Games, the finals of athletics and football competitions, as well as the opening and closing ceremonies of the Beijing 2022 Olympic Winter Games and the XIII Paralympic Winter Games. Covering an area of 204,000 m^2 and a floor area of 258,000 m^2, the stadium can accommodate 91,000 spectators. The stadium is shaped like a "nest" or cradle that nurtures life, embodying humanity's hope for the future.

小结 Summary

1. 听句子选词填空。Listen to the sentences and choose the words to fill in the blanks.  27-03

| A. 校正 | B. 校准 | C. 用力 | D. 尺寸 |

❶ 你会制作尺寸_____件吗？

❷ 重新打开软件，确认_____修改是否合适。

第 27 课 | 校准尺寸

3 把计算出来的_____参数填入相应的 X 校正和 Y 校正的位置。

4 零件比较薄和软的时候，不要太_____。

2. 看词语练拼音。 Look at the words and practice Pinyin.

| chǐcùn | jiàozhǔn | jiàozhèng | yǐjīng |
| 尺寸 | 校准 | 校正 | 已经 |

| fàngpíng | ruǎn | báo | gōngshì |
| 放平 | 软 | 薄 | 公式 |

3. 朗读下列句子。 Read aloud the following sentences.

1 Chóngxīn dǎkāi ruǎnjiàn, quèrèn chǐcùn xiūgǎi shìfǒu héshì.
重新 打开 软件，确认 尺寸 修改 是否 合适。

2 Bǎ jìsuàn chulai de jiàozhèng cānshù tiánrù xiāngyìng de X jiàozhèng hé Y jiàozhèng de wèizhì, diǎnjī "quèdìng" bǎocún.
把 计算 出来 的 校正 参数 填入 相应 的 X 校正 和 Y 校正 的 位置，点击"确定"保存。

第28课 Lesson 28

Duōcéng zhìzào
多层制造
Multi-layer Manufacturing

 复习 Revision

1. 根据图片选择词语。 Choose the words based on the pictures.

❶ 计算（　　）　　❷ 修改（　　）　　❸ 确认（　　）
　 制作（　　）　　　 用力（　　）　　　 打开（　　）

2. 把下列词语组合成短语或句子。 Connect the words into phrases or sentences.

① ①制作　　②件　　③尺寸　　④校准

_____

② ①重新　　②软件　　③打开

_____

第 28 课 | 多层制造

3 ①尺寸   ②确认   ③合适   ④修改

_____

热身 Warm-up

你认识这些词语吗？ Do you know these words?

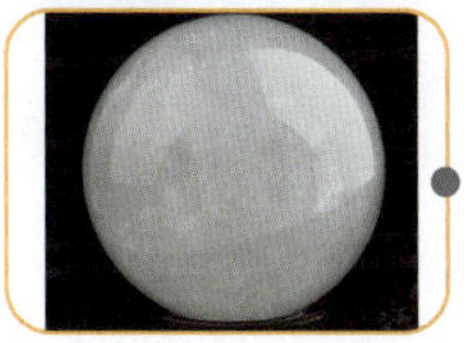

	fāhēi 发黑	blacken
	yánsè 颜色	color
	qiúhuà 球化	spheroidize
	báiliàng 白亮	bright white
	rónghuà 熔化	melt
	tiáoxiǎo 调小	turn down

267

学习生词 Words and Expressions

#	词	拼音	词性	释义
1	单层	dāncéng	*adj.*	single-layer
2	第一层	dì-yī céng	*phr.*	the first layer
3	熔化	rónghuà	*v.*	melt
4	平展	píngzhǎn	*adj.*	flat
5	白亮	báiliàng	*adj.*	bright white
6	颜色	yánsè	*n.*	color
7	若	ruò	*conj.*	if
8	一定	yídìng	*adj.*	certain
9	球化	qiúhuà	*v.*	spheroidize
10	发黑	fāhēi	*phr.*	blacken
11	现象	xiànxiàng	*n.*	phenomenon
12	则	zé	*conj.*	then
13	调小	tiáoxiǎo	*phr.*	turn down
14	效果	xiàoguǒ	*n.*	effect
15	之后	zhīhòu	*n.*	afterwards

第28课 | 多层制造

词语练习 Word Exercises

1. 学习词语搭配。Study the collocations.

❶ xiànxiàng 现象	cháng jiàn xiànxiàng 常见 现象	common phenomenon
	zìrán xiànxiàng 自然 现象	natural phenomenon
❷ dāncéng 单层	dāncéng zhìzào 单层 制造	single-layer manufacturing
	dāncéng shèjì 单层 设计	single-layer design
❸ rónghuà 熔化	kāishǐ rónghuà 开始 熔化	begin to melt
	wánquán rónghuà 完全 熔化	completely melt

2. 给词语选择正确搭配。Choose the right words to form collocations.

❶ dāncéng 单层 _____ 　A. jiégòu 结构　　B. túxíng 图形

❷ píngzhǎn de 平展 的 _____ 　A. píngmiàn 平面　　B. shuǐpíng 水平

❸ báiliàng de 白亮 的 _____ 　A. yánsè 颜色　　B. biǎomiàn 表面

269

学习课文 Text 🎧 28-02

第一步：设定单层制造的高度，然后点击"单层制造"，开始第一层加工。

第二步：观察加工的熔化情况，第一层熔化后应该是平展的平面、白亮的颜色，若有一定的球化、发黑等现象，则需要调小激光功率。

第三步：再次点击"单层制造"，然后观察表面效果是否正常。

第四步：单层制造正常之后，点击"多层制造"按钮开始进行多层制造。

第 28 课 | 多层制造

Step 1: Set the height of single-layer manufacturing, then click "Single-layer manufacturing" to start the processing for the first layer.

Step 2: Observe the melting situation during processing. The first layer should have a flat surface and a bright white color after melting. If there are certain phenomena like spheroidization, blackening, etc., then you need to turn down the laser power.

Step 3: Click "Single-layer manufacturing" again and observe whether the surface effect is normal.

Step 4: After the single-layer manufacturing is normal, click the "Multi-layer manufacturing" button to start the multi-layer manufacturing.

课文练习 Text Exercises

1. 回答问题。Answer the questions.

1. 点击单层制造前，需要设定单层制造的高度吗？
2. 再次点击单层制造后，需要观察表面效果是否正常吗？

2. 根据课文选词填空。Choose the words to fill in the blanks based on the text.

| A. 之后 | B. 第一层 | C. 球化 | D. 平展 |

1. 第一层熔化后应该是_____的平面、白亮的颜色。
2. 单层制造正常_____，点击"多层制造"按钮开始进行多层制造。

学习语法 Grammar

语法点 1　Grammar Point 1

若……，则……　if..., then...

It indicates a hypothetical conditional relationship and is relatively formal. "如果……，就……" can be used in spoken Chinese instead.

1. 若有一定的球化，则需调小激光功率。
2. 若有一定的发黑，则需调小激光功率。
3. 若出现紧急情况，则迅速按下急停开关。

选词填空。Choose the words to fill in the blanks.

A. 若　　　B. 只有

1. _____ 在水冷机运转正常后，才可以打开激光器。
2. _____ 加入金属粉末后，才可以用激光进行逐层扫描。
3. _____ 有一定的球化，则需调小激光功率。
4. _____ 出现紧急情况，则迅速按下急停开关。

语法点 2 Grammar Point 2

副词 "再次"　The adverb "再次"

It indicates the repeated occurrence of an action, behavior, event, or phenomenon.

1. 再次点击"单层制造"。
2. 再次打开软件。
3. 请再次确认尺寸是否合适。

把下列词语组合成短语或句子。Connect the words into phrases or sentences.

1. 设定　　再次　　参数　　打印

　　_____

2. 参数　　计算　　再次　　校正

　　_____

3. 再次　　液位　　升高

　　_____

4. 激光　　再次　　功率　　调小

　　_____

 汉字书写 Writing Chinese Characters

 职业拓展 Career Insight

The resolution of the 3D printer is sufficient for most applications. To obtain objects with higher resolution, the following method can be employed: Use the current 3D printer to first print a slightly larger object, and then perform minor surface polishing to obtain a smooth object with high resolution.

第 28 课 | 多层制造

 小结 Summary

1. 听句子选词填空。 Listen to the sentences and choose the words to fill in the blanks. 🎧 28-03

> A. 单层　　B. 效果　　C. 熔化　　D. 调小

① 观察加工的＿＿＿＿情况。

② 设定＿＿＿＿制造的高度。

③ 观察表面＿＿＿＿是否正常。

④ ＿＿＿＿激光功率。

2. 看词语练拼音。 Look at the words and practice Pinyin.

dāncéng	dì-yī céng	rónghuà	báiliàng
单层	第一层	熔化	白亮
yánsè	tiáoxiǎo	xiàoguǒ	zhīhòu
颜色	调小	效果	之后

3. 朗读下列句子。 Read aloud the following sentences.

① Shèdìng dāncéng zhìzào de gāodù, ránhòu diǎnjī "dāncéng zhìzào", kāishǐ dì-yī céng jiāgōng.
设定 单层 制造的高度，然后点击"单层 制造"，开始第一层加工。

② Ruò yǒu yídìng de qiúhuà、fāhēi děng xiànxiàng, zé xūyào tiáoxiǎo jīguāng gōnglǜ.
若有一定的球化、发黑等 现象，则需要调小 激光 功率。

275

第29课 Lesson 29
Zàntíng hé jìxù jiāgōng
暂停和继续加工
Pausing and Continuing Processing

 复习 Revision

1. 根据图片选择词语。Choose the words based on the pictures.

❶ 调小（　　　）　　❷ 融化（　　　）　　❸ 发黑（　　　）
　 点击（　　　）　　　 平面（　　　）　　　 颜色（　　　）

2. 把下列词语组合成短语或句子。Connect the words into phrases or sentences.

❶ ①设定　②制造　③单层　④高度

　　_____

❷ ①情况　②观察　③熔化　④加工

　　_____

第 29 课 | 暂停和继续加工

3 ①激光　②调小　③功率　④需要

_____

 **热身 Warm-up**

你认识这些词语吗？ Do you know these words?

 停止	tíngzhǐ 停止	stop
 继续	jìxù 继续	continue
 ↑	shàng 上	upper position
 ↓	xià 下	lower position
 (电机)	diànqì 电气	electricity
 ⏸	zàntíng 暂停	pause

277

学习生词 Words and Expressions 🎧 29-01

1	暂停	zàntíng	v.	pause
2	继续	jìxù	v.	continue
3	过程	guòchéng	n.	process
4	暂时	zànshí	adj.	temporary
5	停止	tíngzhǐ	v.	stop
6	前面	qiánmiàn	n.	the preceding part
7	将	jiāng	adv.	will
8	下	xià	n.	lower position
9	想	xiǎng	opt.	want
10	有无	yǒu wú	v.	whether... or not
11	机械	jīxiè	n.	machinery
12	电气	diànqì	n.	electricity
13	一切	yíqiè	pron.	everything
14	都	dōu	adv.	all, both

第 29 课 | 暂停和继续加工

词语练习 Word Exercises

1. 学习词语搭配。Study the collocations.

❶ zànshí 暂时	zànshí zhōngduàn 暂时 中断	temporary interruption
	zànshí tíngliú 暂时 停留	temporarily stay
❷ jīxiè 机械	jīxiè zhìzào 机械 制造	mechanical manufacturing
	jīxiè zhuāngzhì 机械 装置	mechanical device
❸ tíngzhǐ 停止	tíngzhǐ gōngzuò 停止 工作	stop working
	tíngzhǐ zhuàndòng 停止 转动	stop rotating

2. 给词语选择正确搭配。Choose the right words to form collocations.

❶ zàntíng
暂停_____   A. ànniǔ 按钮   B. kòngzhì 控制

❷ diànqì
电气_____   A. xìtǒng 系统   B. jīxiè 机械

❸ tíngzhǐ
停止_____   A. zhìzào 制造   B. shèbèi 设备

学习课文 Text 🎧 29-02

第一步：在自动制造过程中，如果需要暂时停止制造，点击加工控制界面上的"暂停"按钮。

第二步：系统在加工完成前面一层后，将停止加工下一层。

第三步：如果想继续制造，首先检查设备参数是否正常，设备状态有无异常。

第四步：检查机械、电气系统一切都正常后，按下"继续"按钮重新开始制造。

第29课 | 暂停和继续加工

Step 1: In the automatic manufacturing process, if you need to temporarily stop manufacturing, click the "Pause" button on the machining control interface.

Step 2: After processing the previous layer, the system will stop processing the next layer.

Step 3: If you want to continue manufacturing, first check whether the device parameters are normal, and ensure there is no abnormality in the device status.

Step 4: After confirming that everything in the mechanical and electrical systems is normal, press the "Pause" button to restart manufacturing.

课文练习 Text Exercises

1. 回答问题。Answer the questions.

① 你会暂时停止制造吗?

② 如果想继续制造，需要检查设备参数是否正常吗?

2. 根据课文选词填空。Choose the words to fill in the blanks based on the text.

| A. 检查 | B. 暂时 | C. 暂停 | D. 停止 |

① _____ 设备参数是否正常。

② 系统在加工完成前面一层后，将_____加工下一层。

学习语法 Grammar

语法点 1 Grammar Point 1

副词 "将"　　The adverb "将"

It is often used before a verb in written Chinese to indicate that an action or an event will occur soon.

1. 系统在加工完成前面一层后,将停止加工下一层。
2. 结束后,升降台将下降一层高度。
3. 机器控制系统通电后,显示器将开始工作。

选词填空。Choose the words to fill in the blanks.

A. 将　　　　B. 若

1. 系统在加工完成前面一层后,_____停止加工下一层。
2. 结束后,升降台_____下降一层高度。
3. _____有一定的发黑,则需要调小激光功率。
4. _____出现紧急情况,则迅速按下急停开关。

语法点 2 Grammar Point 2

> 副词"都"　The adverb "都"
>
> It indicates "all" or being all-encompassing. Except in interrogative sentences, the components that are encompassed are placed before "都".
>
> 1. 检查一切都正常后,按下"继续"按钮重新开始制造。
> 2. 工业产品、机器零件都可以使用增材制造技术。
> 3. 三个打印参数都设定好了。

给"都"选择正确的位置。Choose the right positions for "都".

1. A 操作设备、连接电线和 B 管道 C 正常。　　　　　(　　)
2. A 检查一切 B 正常后,C 按下"继续"按钮重新开始制造。(　　)
3. A 打印材料 B 准备 C 好了。　　　　　　　　　　　(　　)
4. A 我们 B 学习 C 中文。　　　　　　　　　　　　　(　　)

 **汉字书写** Writing Chinese Characters

zì
自 自 自 自 自 自 自

rú
如 如 如 如 如 如

文化拓展 Culture Insight

China's Space Station, also known as Tiangong or Heavenly Palace, is a national space laboratory constructed by China. It orbits at an altitude of 400–450 kilometers with an inclination angle of 42–43 degrees and has a design lifespan of 10 years. The station can accommodate three taikonauts for extended periods and can be expanded to a maximum configuration of 180 tons and six modules for large-scale space applications. China's Space Station has been opened to international collaboration, promoting the peaceful utilization of space for humanity.

第 29 课 | 暂停和继续加工

 **小结 Summary**

1. 听句子选词填空。Listen to the sentences and choose the words to fill in the blanks. 29-03

> A. 暂时　　B. 暂停　　C. 停止　　D. 正常

❶ 检查设备参数是否_____。

❷ 需要_____停止制造。

❸ 按下"_____"按钮重新开始制造。

❹ _____加工下一层。

2. 看词语练拼音。Look at the words and practice Pinyin.

| zànshí | tíngzhǐ | zàntíng | jìxù |
| 暂时 | 停止 | 暂停 | 继续 |

| qiánmiàn | guòchéng | xiǎng | xià |
| 前面 | 过程 | 想 | 下 |

3. 朗读下列句子。Read aloud the following sentences.

❶ Xìtǒng zài jiāgōng wánchéng qiánmiàn yì céng hòu, jiāng tíngzhǐ jiāgōng xià yì céng.
系统在加工完成前面一层后，将停止加工下一层。

❷ Jiǎnchá jīxiè、diànqì xìtǒng yíqiè dōu zhèngcháng hòu, ànxia "jìxù" ànniǔ chóngxīn kāishǐ zhìzào.
检查机械、电气系统一切都正常后，按下"继续"按钮重新开始制造。

285

第30课 Lesson 30

Qīngjié jīqì
清洁机器
Cleaning the Machine

 复习 Revision

1. 根据图片选择词语。Choose the words based on the pictures.

❶ 自动（　　）　　❷ 继续（　　）　　❸ 上（　　）
　 停止（　　）　　　 按钮（　　）　　　 下（　　）

2. 把下列词语组合成短语或句子。Connect the words into phrases or sentences.

❶ ①停止　②暂时　③制造　④需要

_____

❷ ①停止　②加工　③下一层

_____

第30课 | 清洁机器

3 ①状态　②设备　③异常　④无

_____

 热身 Warm-up

你认识这些词语吗？　Do you know these words?

吸尘器（xīchénqì）		vacuum cleaner
工作服（gōngzuòfú）		work clothes
护目镜（hùmùjìng）		goggles
清洁（qīngjié）		clean
玻璃（bōli）		glass
酒精（jiǔjīng）		(ethyl) alcohol

287

 学习生词 **Words and Expressions**  30-01

1	清洁	qīngjié	*v.*	clean
2	每次	měi cì	*phr.*	each time
3	戴上	dàishang	*phr.*	wear
4	护目镜	hùmùjìng	*n.*	goggles
5	穿好	chuānhǎo	*phr.*	put on
6	工作服	gōngzuòfú	*n.*	work clothes
7	橡胶	xiàngjiāo	*n.*	rubber
8	手套	shǒutào	*n.*	gloves
9	吸尘器	xīchénqì	*n.*	vacuum cleaner
10	内部	nèibù	*n.*	in, inside
11	杂物	záwù	*n.*	sundries
12	棉布	miánbù	*n.*	cotton cloth
13	玻璃	bōli	*n.*	glass
14	酒精	jiǔjīng	*n.*	(ethyl) alcohol
15	小心	xiǎoxīn	*adj.*	careful

第30课 | 清洁机器

词语练习 Word Exercises

1. 学习词语搭配。Study the collocations.

❶ qīngjié 清洁	qīngjié jīqì 清洁 机器	clean the machine
	qīngjié shèbèi 清洁 设备	clean equipment
❷ dàishang 戴上	dàishang hùmùjìng 戴上 护目镜	put on goggles
	dàishang shǒutào 戴上 手套	put on gloves
❸ chuānhǎo 穿好	chuānhǎo gōngzuòfú 穿好 工作服	wear work clothes properly
	chuānhǎo xiézi 穿好 鞋子	wear shoes properly

2. 给词语选择正确搭配。Choose the right words to form collocations.

❶ zhuānyòng 专用_____　　A. shǒutào 手套　　B. dǎkāi 打开

❷ _____ gōngzuò 工作　　A. qīngjié 清洁　　B. nèibù 内部

❸ _____ miánbù 棉布　　A. jiǔjīng 酒精　　B. záwù 杂物

289

 **学习课文 Text** 🎧 30-02

第一步:每次设备打印完成后都必须清洁机器。

第二步:必须先戴上护目镜,穿好工作服,戴上专用橡胶手套,然后再开始清洁工作。

第三步:用毛刷和吸尘器清理机器内部,务必避免机器内部出现螺钉、工具等杂物。

第四步:用棉布清洁玻璃和机器外壳。

第五步:用酒精棉布小心清洁护目镜等工具。

第 30 课 | 清洁机器

Step 1: Clean the machine every time after the device completes printing.

Step 2: Wear goggles, put on work clothes, and wear special rubber gloves before starting the cleaning work.

Step 3: Use a brush and a vacuum cleaner to clean the inside of the machine. Be sure to avoid the existence of screws, tools and other sundries inside the machine.

Step 4: Clean the glass and machine shell with a cotton cloth.

Step 5: Carefully clean the goggles and other tools with an alcohol cotton cloth.

课文练习 Text Exercises

1. 回答问题。Answer the questions.

① 每次打印完成后都要清洁机器吗？

② 清洁机器时需要戴上护目镜和专用橡胶手套吗？

2. 根据课文选词填空。Choose the words to fill in the blanks based on the text.

A. 吸尘器	B. 护目镜	C. 主机	D. 酒精

① 清洁机器时必须戴上_____。

② 用毛刷和_____清理机器内部。

学习语法 Grammar

语法点1 Grammar Point 1

代词"每" The pronoun "每"

It is used before a noun or a measure word to indicate any one or part of the whole.

1. 每次设备打印完成后都必须清洁机器。
2. 每个参数都很重要。
3. 每个步骤我都会操作。

选词填空。Choose the words to fill in the blanks.

A. 每　　B. 都

1. _____次设备打印完成后_____必须清洁机器。
2. _____个参数_____很重要。
3. 我_____天按时上课。
4. 三个打印参数_____设定好了。

语法点 2 Grammar Point 2

副词"必须"　The adverb "必须"

It is used before a verb to indicate necessity in terms of both the reason and rationality.

1. 每次设备打印完成后都必须清洁机器。
2. 打印模型前，必须进行预处理吗？
3. 文件必须保存为 STL 格式。

把下列词语组合成短语或句子。Connect the words into phrases or sentences.

1. 文件　必须　将　转换　格式　为　STL　格式

___

2. 必须　校正　正确　参数　计算

___

3. 添加　打印　以前　必须　模型　支撑

___

4. 一定　若　球化　有　的，必须　功率　激光　调小

___

 ## 汉字书写 Writing Chinese Characters

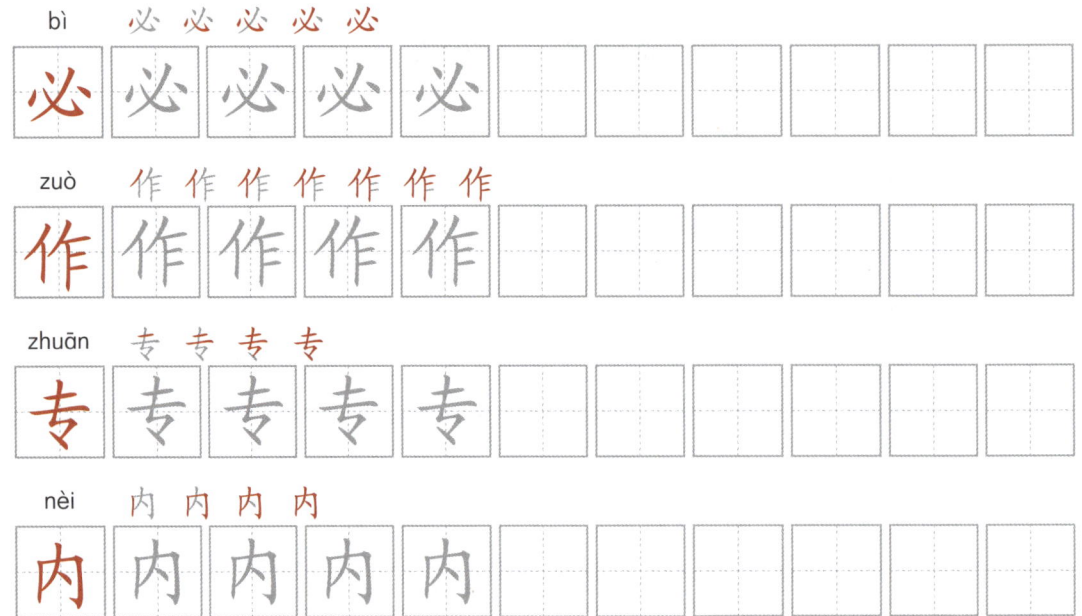

 ## 职业拓展 Career Insight

Use a combination of alcohol and non-woven fabric to wipe out the dust inside the device. Do not use a damp cloth in order to prevent water from seeping into the motherboard and causing a short circuit. Alcohol is a good organic solvent that dissolves stains without causing a short circuit of the device.

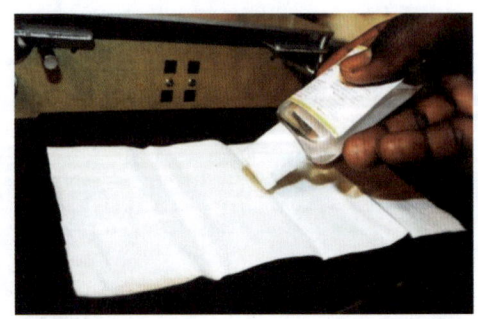

第 30 课 | 清洁机器

 **小结 Summary**

1. 听句子选词填空。 Listen to the sentences and choose the words to fill in the blanks. 🎧 30-03

> A. 内部　　B. 小心　　C. 玻璃　　D. 每次

1 用酒精棉布_____清洁护目镜。

2 用棉布清洁_____和机器外壳。

3 用毛刷和吸尘器清理机器_____。

4 _____设备打印完成后都必须清洁机器。

2. 看词语练拼音。 Look at the words and practice Pinyin.

| qīngjié | xiàngjiāo | gōngzuòfú | miánbù |
| 清洁 | 橡胶 | 工作服 | 棉布 |

| xiǎoxīn | jiǔjīng | bōli | nèibù |
| 小心 | 酒精 | 玻璃 | 内部 |

3. 朗读下列句子。 Read aloud the following sentences.

1 Bìxū xiān dàishang hùmùjìng, chuānhǎo gōngzuòfú, dàishang zhuānyòng xiàngjiāo shǒutào.
　必须 先 戴上 护目镜，穿好 工作服，戴上 专用 橡胶 手套。

2 Wùbì bìmiǎn jīqì nèibù chūxiàn luódīng、gōngjù děng záwù.
　务必 避免 机器 内部 出现 螺钉、工具 等 杂物。

295

第31课 Lesson 31

Jiǎnchá jīqì
检查机器
Checking the Machine

 复习 Revision

1. 根据图片选择词语。 Choose the words based on the pictures.

① 吸尘器（　　）　　② 酒精（　　）　　③ 工作服（　　）
　 计算机（　　）　　　 玻璃（　　）　　　 护目镜（　　）

2. 把下列词语组合成短语或句子。 Connect the words into phrases or sentences.

① ①必须　②机器　③清洁　④每次

_____

② ①橡胶　②手套　③戴上　④专用

_____

第31课 | 检查机器

3 ①内部   ②出现   ③避免   ④杂物

_____

热身 Warm-up

你认识这些词语吗？ Do you know these words?

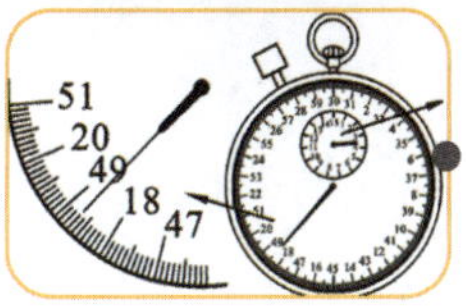

	qìtǐ 气体	gas
	lěngquèshuǐ 冷却水	cooling water
	xúnhuán 循环	circulate
	liúdòng 流动	flow
	qìyābiǎo 气压表	barometer
	dúshù 读数	reading

297

 学习生词 Words and Expressions  31-01

1	主机	zhǔjī	n.	host (machine)
2	之间	zhījiān	n.	space between things/people
3	进气口	jìnqìkǒu	n.	air inlet
4	通入	tōngrù	phr.	inject
5	气体	qìtǐ	n.	gas
6	冷却水	lěngquèshuǐ	n.	cooling water
7	循环	xúnhuán	v.	circulate
8	流动	liúdòng	v.	flow
9	气压表	qìyābiǎo	n.	barometer
10	读数	dúshù	n.	reading
11	此外	cǐwài	conj.	in addition
12	还	hái	adv.	also
13	要	yào	opt.	need to
14	完好	wánhǎo	adj.	intact
15	松动	sōngdòng	v.	come loose

第31课 | 检查机器

词语练习 Word Exercises

1. 学习词语搭配。Study the collocations.

① tōngrù 通入	tōngrù qìtǐ 通入 气体	inject gas
	tōngrù yètǐ 通入 液体	inject liquid
② xúnhuán 循环	xúnhuán liúdòng 循环 流动	circular flow
	chóngfù xúnhuán 重复 循环	repetitive cycle
③ sōngdòng 松动	liánjiē sōngdòng 连接 松动	loose connection
	shèbèi sōngdòng 设备 松动	loose equipment

2. 给词语选择正确搭配。Choose the right words to form collocations.

① liánjiē 连接_____　A. zhǔjī 主机　B. zhījiān 之间

② _____ bǎohù 保护　A. qìtǐ 气体　B. yètǐ 液体

③ _____ zhèngcháng 正常　A. dúshù 读数　B. yánsè 颜色

学习课文 Text 🎧 31-02

第一步: 首先检查主机和电脑之间是否已经连接,进气口是否通入气体,然后检查激光器是否有冷却水循环流动。

第二步: 检查气压表读数是否正常。

第三步: 检查外观是否变形,开启和关闭激光头是否正常,此外,还要检查密封胶圈是否完好等。

第四步: 不仅要检查缸体是否松动,还要检查主机内部是否遗落其他物体。

第 31 课 | 检查机器

Step 1: First, check whether the host and the computer are connected, whether the gas is injected into the air inlet, and then check whether there is a circular flow of cooling water in the laser.

Step 2: Check whether the barometer reading is normal.

Step 3: Check whether there is any deformation in the appearance, and whether the laser head can be turned on or off normally. In addition, check whether the sealing rubber ring is intact, etc.

Step 4: Check not only whether the cylinder body is loose, but also whether there are any other objects left inside the host.

课文练习 Text Exercises

1. 回答问题。Answer the questions.

① 需要检查主机和电脑之间是否已经连接吗?

② 需要检查气压表读数是否正常吗?

2. 根据课文选词填空。Choose the words to fill in the blanks based on the text.

> A. 完好   B. 读数   C. 还要   D. 流动

① 还要检查密封胶圈是否_____等。

② _____检查主机内部是否遗落其他物体。

学习语法 Grammar

语法点 1 Grammar Point 1

连词"此外" The conjunction "此外"

It indicates things in addition to what was mentioned above.

1. 此外，还要检查密封胶圈是否完好等。
2. 操作前要穿工作服，此外，还要戴安全帽、防护手套、护目镜等。
3. 增材制造技术可以制造工业产品，此外，还可以制造生物产品。

选词填空。Choose the words to fill in the blanks.

A. 此外   B. 其他

1. _____，还要检查密封胶圈是否完好等。
2. 我会打开软件，_____操作不会。
3. 操作前要穿工作服，_____，还要戴安全帽、防护手套、护目镜等。
4. 增材制造技术可以用在工业领域，还可以用在_____领域吗？

第31课 | 检查机器

 语法点 2 **Grammar Point 2**

不仅……，还……　not only..., but also...

It indicates a progressive relationship.

1. 不仅要检查缸体是否松动，还要检查主机内部是否遗落其他物体。
2. 增材制造技术不仅可以用在工业领域，还可以制造生物产品。
3. 我不仅会创建文件，还会保存文件。

选词填空。Choose the words to fill in the blanks.

A. 不仅　　　　B. 如果

1. _____要检查缸体是否松动，还要检查主机内部是否遗落其他物体。
2. _____第一层加工正常，就进行后续多层制造。
3. _____水冷机运转正常，就可以打开激光器。
4. 增材制造技术_____可以制造工业产品，还可以制造生物产品。

 **汉字书写** **Writing Chinese Characters**

qì
气 气 气 气
气 气 气 气 气

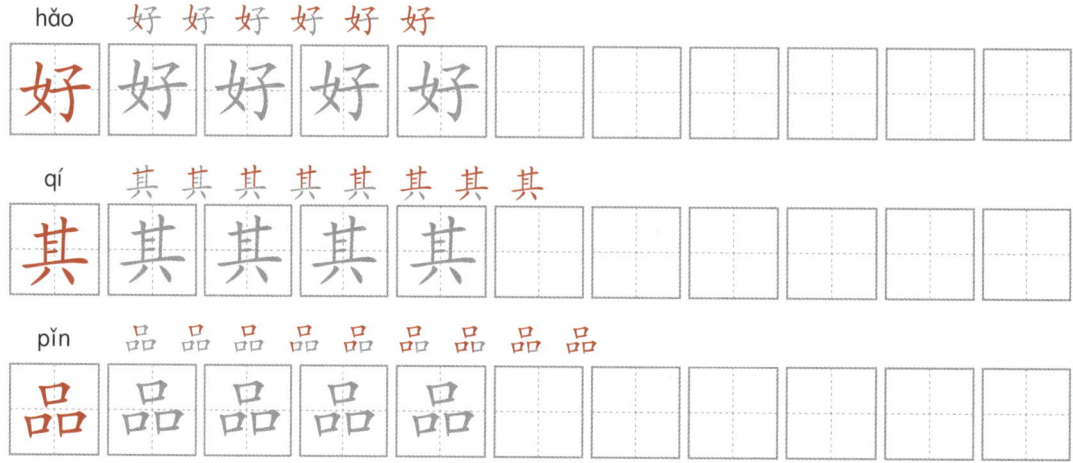

 文化拓展 Culture Insight

The fifth-generation mobile communication technology, abbreviated as 5G, is a new broadband mobile communication technology characterized by high speed, low latency, and massive connectivity. As a new type of mobile communication network, 5G addresses the challenges of human-to-machine and machine-to-machine communication while meeting the demands of IoT applications such as mobile healthcare, the Internet of Vehicles, smart homes, and industrial control. With the world's largest and most advanced 5G network, China has made significant contributions to the development of 5G standards and has conducted extensive explorations in industry application standards.

第 31 课 | 检查机器

 **小结 Summary**

1. 听句子选词填空。Listen to the sentences and choose the words to fill in the blanks. 🎧 31-03

| A. 之间 | B. 冷却水 | C. 其他 | D. 进气口 |

❶ 激光器是否有_____循环流动。

❷ _____是否通入气体。

❸ 内部是否遗落_____物品。

❹ 检查主机和电脑_____是否已经连接。

2. 看词语练拼音。Look at the words and practice Pinyin.

| cǐwài | xúnhuán | dúshù | tōngrù |
| 此外 | 循环 | 读数 | 通入 |

| lěngquèshuǐ | qìyābiǎo | sōngdòng | qítā |
| 冷却水 | 气压表 | 松动 | 其他 |

3. 朗读下列句子。Read aloud the following sentences.

❶ Ránhòu jiǎnchá jīguāngqì shìfǒu yǒu lěngquèshuǐ xúnhuán liúdòng.
然后 检查 激光器 是否 有 冷却水 循环 流动。

❷ Jiǎnchá wàiguān shìfǒu biànxíng, kāiqǐ hé guānbì jīguāngtóu shìfǒu zhèngcháng.
检查 外观 是否 变形，开启 和 关闭 激光头 是否 正常。

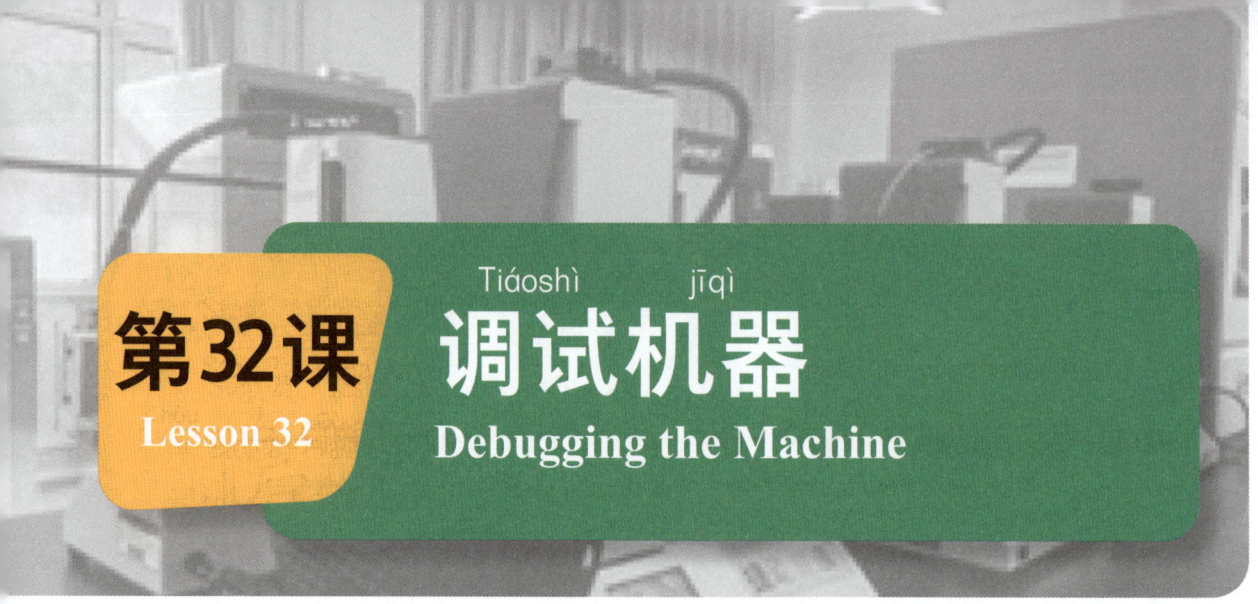

第32课 Lesson 32

调试机器 (Tiáoshì jīqì)
Debugging the Machine

 复习 Revision

1. 根据图片选择词语。 Choose the words based on the pictures.

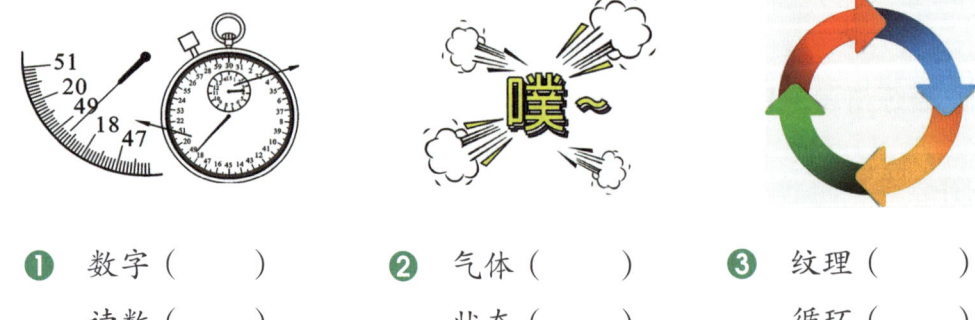

❶ 数字（　　）　　❷ 气体（　　）　　❸ 纹理（　　）
　 读数（　　）　　　 状态（　　）　　　 循环（　　）

2. 把下列词语组合成短语或句子。 Connect the words into phrases or sentences.

① ①读数　②正常　③是否　④气压表

_____

② ①是否　②密封　③胶圈　④完好

_____

第 32 课 | 调试机器

3　①内部　②物体　③是否　④遗落

_____

 **热身 Warm-up**

你认识这些词语吗？ Do you know these words?

所有 图片	suǒyǒu 所有	all
工作缸 图片	gōngzuògāng 工作缸	working cylinder
前后 图片	qiánhòu 前后	back and forth
窗口 图片	chuāngkǒu 窗口	window
仪表 图片	yíbiǎo 仪表	instrument
钢板 图片	gāngbǎn 钢板	steel plate

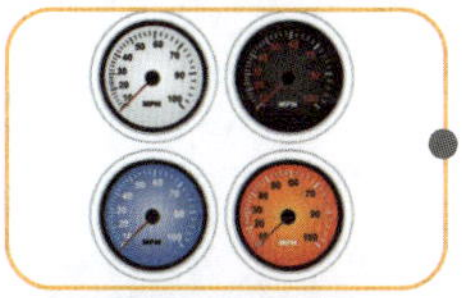

307

学习生词 Words and Expressions  32-01

1	上述	shàngshù	*adj.*	above-mentioned
2	所有	suǒyǒu	*adj.*	all
3	就绪	jiùxù	*v.*	(be) ready
4	工作缸	gōngzuògāng	*n.*	working cylinder
5	至	zhì	*v.*	(get) to
6	处	chù	*n.*	place
7	前后	qiánhòu	*n.*	back and forth
8	有效	yǒuxiào	*v.*	(be) valid
9	窗口	chuāngkǒu	*n.*	window
10	仪表	yíbiǎo	*n.*	instrument
11	钢板	gāngbǎn	*n.*	steel plate
12	最后	zuìhòu	*n.*	(in time/sequence) the last
13	调入	diàorù	*phr.*	transfer... to...

第 32 课 | 调试机器

 词语练习 Word Exercises

1. 学习词语搭配。Study the collocations.

❶ suǒyǒu 所有	suǒyǒu wénjiàn 所有 文件	all the files
	suǒyǒu jīqì 所有 机器	all the machines
❷ chuāngkǒu 窗口	shèbèi chuāngkǒu 设备 窗口	device window
	ruǎnjiàn chuāngkǒu 软件 窗口	software window
❸ diàorù 调入	diàorù shùjù 调入 数据	import the data
	diàorù cānshù 调入 参数	import the parameters

2. 给词语选择正确搭配。Choose the right words to form collocations.

❶ bùzhòu 步骤_____　　A. qiánhòu 前后　　B. jiùxù 就绪

❷ guānchá 观察_____　　A. yíbiǎo 仪表　　B. gōngshì 公式

❸ _____ gōngzuògāng 工作缸　　A. guòchéng 过程　　B. jiǎnchá 检查

309

学习课文 Text 🎧 32-02

第一步：上述所有步骤就绪后，先调试好工作缸和铺粉系统，再将底板上升至距离基准面 25 mm 处。

第二步：点击按钮，前后移动铺粉装置，观察是否正常。如果没有移动，则检查参数设置是否有效。

第三步：打开加热功能窗口，检查加热仪表显示是否正常，5 分钟后检查钢板是否已经加热。

第四步：最后将准备加工的 STL 文件调入计算机。

第32课 | 调试机器

Step 1: After all the above steps are ready, first debug the working cylinder and powder-spreading system, and then raise the base plate to a position 25 mm away from the datum plane.

Step 2: Click the button to move the powder-spreading device back and forth, and observe whether it is normal. If it doesn't move, check whether the parameter settings are valid.

Step 3: Open the window of the heating function and check whether the heating instrument displays normally. After 5 minutes, check whether the steel plate has been heated.

Step 4: Finally, transfer the STL file prepared for processing to the computer.

课文练习 Text Exercises

1. 回答问题。Answer the questions.

① 需要将底板上升至距离基准面 25mm 处吗？

② 是否需要打开加热功能，检查加热仪表是否正常？

2. 根据课文选词填空。Choose the words to fill in the blanks based on the text.

> A. 所有　　　B. 有效　　　C. 最后　　　D. 就绪

① 上述所有步骤_____后，先调试好工作缸和铺粉系统。

② 检查参数设置是否_____。

学习语法 Grammar

语法点 1　Grammar Point 1

形容词"所有"　The adjective "所有"

It indicates "all, with no exception". The structure is: 所有 + noun.

1. 上述所有步骤就绪后，先调试好工作缸和铺粉系统。
2. 所有步骤我都会操作了。
3. 所有打印材料都准备好了。

选词填空。Choose the words to fill in the blanks.

　　　　　　　　A. 所有　　　　B. 都

1. 检查一切_____正常后，按下"继续"按钮重新开始制造。
2. 上述_____步骤结束后，先调试工作缸和铺粉系统。
3. 工业领域、生物领域_____可以使用增材制造技术。
4. _____设备参数一切正常。

语法点 2　Grammar Point 2

动词 + 至 + 地点　Verb + 至 + place

It indicates the endpoint of a movement and is often used in written Chinese. In spoken Chinese, "verb + 至 + place" is often used instead.

第 32 课 | 调试机器

❶ 将底板上升至距离基准面 25mm 处。

❷ 将工作缸底板上升至基准面以上。

❸ 将模型文件保存至工作界面。

选词填空。 Choose the words to fill in the blanks.

A. 至　　　　B. 直到

❶ 将底板上升_____距离基准面 25mm 处。

❷ 重复上一个步骤，_____整个成型结束。

❸ 将模型文件保存_____工作界面。

❹ 重复前面的步骤，_____模型打印完成。

 汉字书写 Writing Chinese Characters

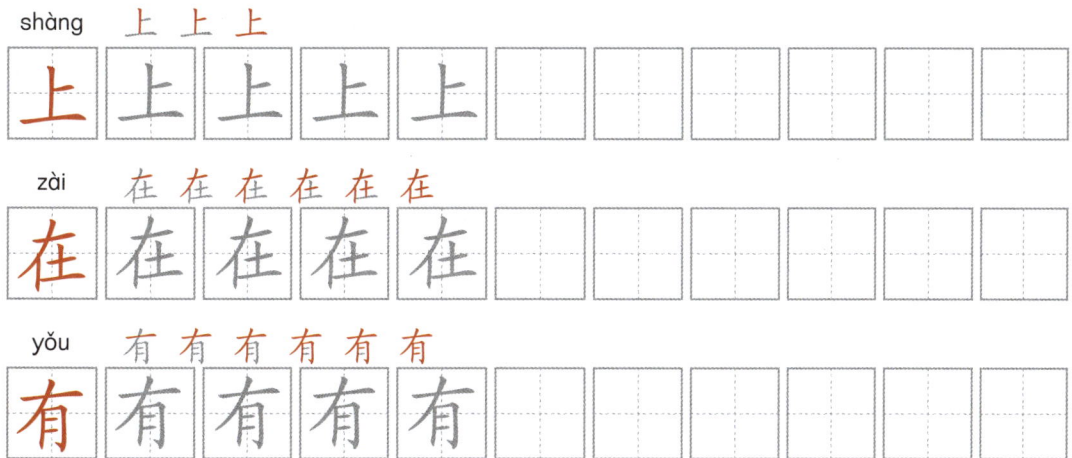

gōng 工 工 工

工 工 工 工 工

职业拓展 Career Insight

The metal printing process encompasses design, preprocessing, printing, and quality inspection. When these processes are mastered proficiently, high-precision and low-cost metal products can be efficiently manufactured. This technology is applicable to engine nozzles in the aviation industry, as it utilizes titanium alloy materials, offers high printing precision, and ensures reliable quality. The hardness test result is 240 HV, significantly higher than the 182 HV achieved through traditional methods.

小结 Summary

1. 听句子选词填空。**Listen to the sentences and choose the words to fill in the blanks.** 32-03

| A. 最后 | B. 好 | C. 就绪 | D. 处 |

第 32 课 ｜ 调试机器

1️⃣ 先调试_____工作缸和铺粉系统。

2️⃣ 上述所有步骤_____后，先调试好工作缸和铺粉系统。

3️⃣ 再将底板上升至距离基准面 25mm_____。

4️⃣ _____将准备加工的 STL 文件调入计算机。

2. 看词语练拼音。Look at the words and practice Pinyin.

shàngshù	yǒuxiào	zuìhòu	zhì
上述	有效	最后	至

gōngzuògāng	yíbiǎo	gāngbǎn	shēngjiàng
工作缸	仪表	钢板	升降

3. 朗读下列句子。Read aloud the following sentences.

1️⃣ Rúguǒ méiyǒu yídòng, zé jiǎnchá cānshù shèzhì shìfǒu yǒuxiào.
如果 没有 移动，则 检查 参数 设置 是否 有效。

2️⃣ Dǎkāi jiārè gōngnéng chuāngkǒu, jiǎnchá jiārè yíbiǎo xiǎnshì shìfǒu zhèngcháng.
打开 加热 功能 窗口，检查 加热 仪表 显示 是否 正常。

第33课 Lesson 33

Shèbèi tíshìyǔ
设备提示语
Equipment Prompts

 复习 Revision

1. 根据图片选择词语。Choose the words based on the pictures.

① 速度（　　）　　② 窗口（　　）　　③ 进气口（　　）
　 仪表（　　）　　　 杂物（　　）　　　 工作缸（　　）

2. 把下列词语组合成短语或句子。Connect the words into phrases or sentences.

① ①按钮　　②移动　　③前后　　④点击

＿＿＿＿＿＿＿＿＿＿＿＿＿＿＿＿＿＿＿＿＿＿＿＿＿

② ①打开　　②窗口　　③加热　　④功能

＿＿＿＿＿＿＿＿＿＿＿＿＿＿＿＿＿＿＿＿＿＿＿＿＿

316

3. ①设置 ②有效 ③是否 ④参数

_____

热身 Warm-up

你认识这些词语吗？ Do you know these words?

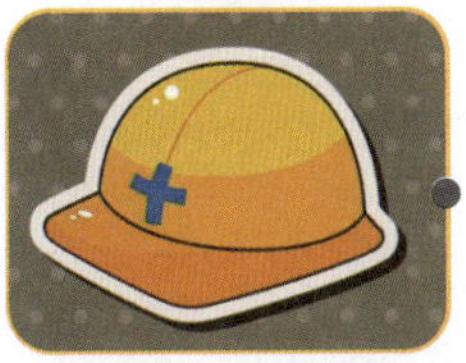

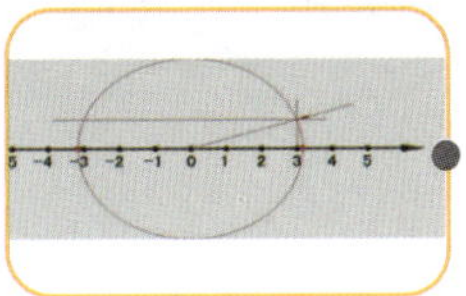

笔记本电脑	chūshǐhuà 初始化	initialize
警告标志	jǐnggào 警告	warn
人物	qǐng 请	please
安全帽	ānquán 安全	safe
奖章	chénggōng 成功	succeed
数轴	yuándiǎn 原点	origin

 学习生词 **Words and Expressions**  33-01

1	提示语	tíshìyǔ	n.	prompt
2	初始化	chūshǐhuà	v.	initialize
3	失败	shībài	v.	fail
4	C轴	C zhóu	phr.	C-axis
5	警告	jǐnggào	v.	warn
6	请	qǐng	v.	please
7	安全	ānquán	adj.	safe
8	单击	dānjī	v.	click
9	使	shǐ	v.	make, cause
10	回到	huídào	v.	return
11	原点	yuándiǎn	n.	origin
12	超出	chāochū	v.	exceed
13	成功	chénggōng	v.	succeed

第 33 课 | 设备提示语

词语练习 Word Exercises

1. 学习词语搭配。Study the collocations.

❶ ānquán 安全	ānquán quèrèn 安全 确认	safety confirmation
	ānquán jùlí 安全 距离	safe distance
❷ huídào 回到	huídào yuándiǎn 回到 原点	return to the origin
	huídào zhōngjiān 回到 中间	return to the middle
❸ chāochū 超出	chāochū fànwéi 超出 范围	out of range
	chāochū qūyù 超出 区域	beyond the area

2. 给词语选择正确搭配。Choose the right words to form collocations.

❶ yìngjiàn
硬件_____   A. chūshǐhuà 初始化   B. móshì 模式

❷ _____shībài
失败   A. dǎyìn 打印   B. shèzhì 设置

❸ _____ànjiàn
按键   A. shìfǒu 是否   B. dānjī 单击

学习课文 Text 🎧 33-02

1. Yìngjiàn chūshǐhuà shībài.
   硬件 初始化 失败。

2. Dǎkāi / bǎocún wénjiàn shībài!
   打开/保存 文件 失败!

3. Shèzhì C zhóu cānshù shībài!
   设置 C 轴 参数 失败!

4. Wú dǎyìn shùjù!
   无 打印 数据!

5. Jǐnggào! Qǐng jiāng Z zhóu yí zhì ānquán wèizhì!
   警告! 请 将 Z 轴 移至安全位置!

6. Qǐng dānjī HOME jiàn shǐ C zhóu、Z zhóu jí R zhóu
   请 单击 HOME 键 使 C 轴、Z 轴 及 R 轴
   huídào yuándiǎn.
   回到 原点。

7. Língjiàn chāochū dǎyìn fànwéi!
   零件 超出 打印 范围!

8. Língjiàn chóngdié!
   零件 重叠!

9. Dǎyìn zhōng! Shìfǒu yào tíngzhǐ dǎyìn?
   打印 中! 是否 要 停止 打印?

10. Qǐng guānbì qiánmén!
    请 关闭 前门!

第 33 课 | 设备提示语

11. Yǐ zàntíng dǎyìn!
    已 暂停 打印!

12. Dǎyìn chénggōng!
    打印 成功!

1. Hardware initialization failed!

2. File opening/saving failed!

3. C-axis parameter setting failed!

4. Printing data not available!

5. Warning! Move the Z-axis to a safe position!

6. Click HOME to make the C-axis, Z-axis, and R-axis return to the origin.

7. The part exceeds the printing range!

8. The parts overlapped!

9. Printing! Do you want to stop the printing?

10. Close the front door!

11. Printing suspended!

12. Printing successful!

课文练习 Text Exercises

1. 回答问题。Answer the questions.

   ① 零件可以超出打印范围吗?

   ② 停止打印后是否要将前门关闭?

2. 根据课文选词填空。Choose the words to fill in the blanks based on the text.

> A. 超出　　　B. 失败　　　C. 安全　　　D. 单击

① 设置 C 轴参数_____！

② 请_____HOME 键使 C 轴、Z 轴及 R 轴回到原点。

学习语法 Grammar

 语法点 1　Grammar Point 1

> **连词"及"**　The conjunction "及"
>
> 　　It is often used in written Chinese to connect juxtaposed words or phrases and can also be expressed as "以及".
>
> ① 使 C 轴、Z 轴及 R 轴回到原点。
> ② 打印参数有层厚、壁厚及移动距离。
> ③ 操作前要戴安全帽、防护手套及护目镜等。

选词填空。Choose the words to fill in the blanks.

> A. 及　　　　　　　　　B. 即

① 壁厚_____模型外壳厚度。

第 33 课 | 设备提示语

② 使 C 轴、Z 轴_____R 轴回到原点。

③ 打印参数有层厚、壁厚_____移动距离。

④ 层厚_____切片厚度。

语法点 2 Grammar Point 2

方位词 "中" The word of location "中"

It is used after a verb to indicate a continuous state. The common structure is: (在+) verb + 中.

① 打印中！

② 开机中！

③ 设备在运行中。

选词填空。Choose the words to fill in the blanks.

| A. 中 | B. 下 |

① 按_____按钮。　　　② 按_____开关。

③ 打印_____！　　　　④ 关机_____！

323

 汉字书写 Writing Chinese Characters

 文化拓展 Culture Insight

Chinese characters are the written symbols of the Chinese language and belong to the category of morphemic and syllabic characters within the ideographic system. They are also among the oldest scripts in the world, with a history of approximately 6,000 years. Chinese characters have been continuously used for the longest time and are the sole surviving inheritor of various ancient writing systems. Throughout the Chinese history, Chinese characters have been regarded as the primary official script.

第 33 课 | 设备提示语

 小结 Summary

1. 听句子选词填空。Listen to the sentences and choose the words to fill in the blanks. 🎧 33-03

> A. 失败　　B. 成功　　C. 超出　　D. 请

❶ 打开/保存文件_____！　　　❷ _____关闭前门！

❸ 零件_____打印范围！　　　❹ 打印_____！

2. 看词语练拼音。Look at the words and practice Pinyin.

| tíshìyǔ | C zhóu | shìfǒu | shǐ |
| 提示语 | C 轴 | 是否 | 使 |

| yuándiǎn | qǐng | tuìchū | chénggōng |
| 原点 | 请 | 退出 | 成功 |

3. 朗读下列句子。Read aloud the following sentences.

❶ Jǐnggào! Qǐng jiāng Z zhóu yí zhì ānquán wèizhì!
　警告！请 将 Z 轴 移至 安全 位置！

❷ Dǎyìn zhōng! Shìfǒu yào tuìchū dǎyìn?
　打印 中！是否 要 退出 打印？

325

第34课 Lesson 34
注意安全 Zhùyì ānquán
Safety Precautions

 复习 Revision

1. 根据图片选择词语。Choose the words based on the pictures.

① 警告（　　）　　② 失败（　　）　　③ 请（　　）
　 安全（　　）　　　 成功（　　）　　　 使（　　）

2. 把下列词语组合成短语或句子。Connect the words into phrases or sentences.

① ①是否　②要　③打印　④退出

_____

② ①失败　②文件　③打开/保存

_____

326

第 34 课 | 注意安全

3 ①超出　②打印　③范围　④零件

_____

 热身 Warm-up

你认识这些词语吗？ Do you know these words?

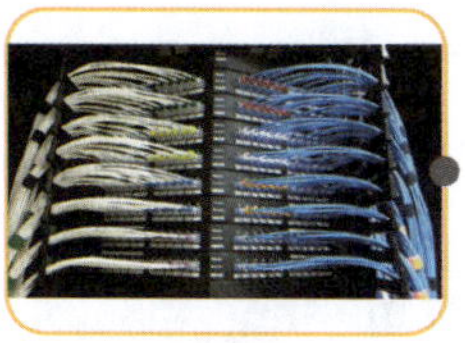	bùxiàn 布线	wire
	mièhuǒqì 灭火器	fire extinguisher
	zhàomíng 照明	light, illuminate
	fēngshàn 风扇	fan
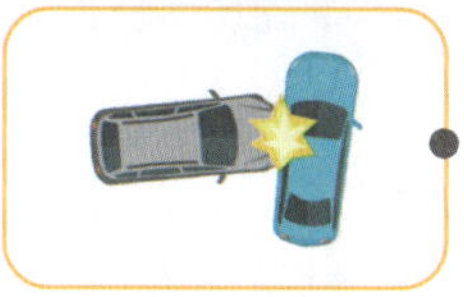	shìgù 事故	accident
	ānquánmào 安全帽	safety helmet

327

学习生词 Words and Expressions  34-01

1	注意	zhù//yì	v.	precaution
2	严格	yángé	adj.	strict
3	布线	bùxiàn	v.	wire
4	防火	fánghuǒ	v.	prevent fires
5	灭火器	mièhuǒqì	n.	fire extinguisher
6	厂房	chǎngfáng	n.	factory building
7	防爆	fángbào	v.	be explosion-proof
8	照明	zhàomíng	v.	light, illuminate
9	以免	yǐmiǎn	conj.	lest
10	聚集	jùjí	v.	accumulate
11	事故	shìgù	n.	accident
12	风扇	fēngshàn	n.	fan
13	培训	péixùn	v.	train
14	安全帽	ānquánmào	n.	safety helmet
15	装备	zhuāngbèi	n.	gear, equipment

第34课 | 注意安全

词语练习 Word Exercises

1. 学习词语搭配。Study the collocations.

❶ yángé 严格	yángé kòngzhì 严格 控制	strictly control
	yángé yāoqiú 严格 要求	strictly require
❷ péixùn 培训	ānquán péixùn 安全 培训	safety training
	jìnxíng péixùn 进行 培训	conduct training
❸ zhuāngbèi 装备	ānquán zhuāngbèi 安全 装备	safety equipment
	fánghuǒ zhuāngbèi 防火 装备	fire prevention equipment

2. 给词语选择正确搭配。Choose the right words to form collocations.

❶ zhùyì 注意_____   A. ānquán 安全   B. jùjí 聚集

❷ bǎifàng 摆放_____   A. mièhuǒqì 灭火器   B. bùxiàn 布线

❸ _____shèbèi 设备   A. fángbào 防爆   B. chǎngfáng 厂房

学习课文 Text 🎧 34-02

1. 设备安装的时候，必须严格按照安全要求进行机器摆放和布线。

2. 按照防火安全要求，在相应位置摆放灭火器。

3. 厂房必须安装防爆照明设备。

4. 为了确保厂房通风，以免粉末聚集，出现安全事故，应该安装防爆风扇。

5. 为了避免出现安全事故，必须进行安全培训。

6. 操作前戴好安全帽、手套、护目镜等安全装备。

1. When installing the device, conduct machine placement and wiring strictly following the safety requirements.
2. Place fire extinguishers in the corresponding positions following the fireproof safety requirements.
3. Lighting devices installed in the factory building must be explosion-proof.
4. In order to ensure ventilation in the factory building and to avoid powder accumulation and safety accidents, explosion-proof fans should be installed.
5. Safety training must be conducted to avoid safety accidents.
6. Wear safety helmets, gloves, goggles and other safety gears before the operation.

课文练习 Text Exercises

1. 回答问题。Answer the questions.

① 必须进行安全培训吗？

② 厂房需要通风并安装防爆风扇吗？

2. 根据课文选词填空。Choose the words to fill in the blanks based on the text.

| A. 以免 | B. 防火 | C. 安全帽 | D. 培训 |

① 按照_____安全要求，在相应位置摆放灭火器。

② 操作前戴好_____、手套、护目镜等安全装备。

 学习语法 Grammar

 语法点1 Grammar Point 1

介词"为了" The preposition "为了"

It indicates the purpose of an action. The common structure is: 为了 + purpose, + action.

1. 为了避免出现安全事故，必须进行安全培训。
2. 为了防止模型发生变形，应该先添加支撑。
3. 为了建立物体的三维模型，需要获取物体表面大量密集的数据信息。

选词填空。Choose the words to fill in the blanks.

A. 为了   B. 便于

1. _____避免出现安全事故，必须进行安全培训。
2. _____防止模型发生变形，应该先添加支撑。
3. 把材料加热到液体状态，_____凝固形成实物。
4. 把升降台下降一层高度，_____进行第二层扫描。

语法点 2 Grammar Point 2

连词"以免" The conjunction "以免"

It is used at the beginning of the second clause and means that if you have done what was mentioned in the first clause, you can avoid the adverse situations that may arise later. It is often used in written Chinese.

1. 确保通风，以免粉末聚集。
2. 必须保证粉末是干燥的，以免氧化。
3. 打印前务必添加支撑，以免模型发生变形。

选词填空。Choose the words to fill in the blanks.

A. 以免   B. 确保

1. 必须保证粉末是干燥的，_____氧化。
2. _____粉末顶部是铺平的。
3. 打印前务必添加支撑，_____模型发生变形。
4. _____第一层粉末是均匀的。

汉字书写 Writing Chinese Characters

bù 布 布 布 布 布 布

 职业拓展 Career Insight

In our daily lives, we must use electrical devices correctly, avoid unauthorized wiring and improper socket placement, refrain from excessive electricity use, replace aging electrical devices and circuits promptly, and turn off power switches when leaving a room. During the cold winter months, prioritize fire and electrical safety, especially during the heating season, and promptly remove surrounding combustible materials. Do not forget to turn off the power and gas switches when going out.

第 34 课 | 注意安全

 小结 Summary

1. 听句子选词填空。Listen to the sentences and choose the words to fill in the blanks. 34-03

> A. 事故　　B. 聚集　　C. 防爆　　D. 严格

1 厂房必须安装_____照明设备。

2 为了避免出现安全_____，必须进行安全培训。

3 为了确保厂房通风，以免粉末_____，应该安装防爆风扇。

4 必须_____按照安全要求进行机器摆放和布线。

2. 看词语练拼音。Look at the words and practice Pinyin.

bùxiàn	chǎngfáng	yǐmiǎn	mièhuǒqì
布线	厂房	以免	灭火器
ānquánmào	zhàomíng	péixùn	zhuāngbèi
安全帽	照明	培训	装备

3. 朗读下列句子。Read aloud the following sentences.

1 Chǎngfáng bìxū ānzhuāng fángbào zhàomíng shèbèi.
　厂房　必须　安装　防爆　照明　设备。

2 Wèile bìmiǎn chūxiàn ānquán shìgù, bìxū jìnxíng ānquán péixùn.
　为了　避免　出现　安全　事故，必须　进行　安全　培训。

第35课 Lesson 35

Bǎoyǎng shèbèi
保养设备
Equipment Maintenance

 复习 Revision

1. 根据图片选择词语。Choose the words based on the pictures.

❶ 安全帽（　　）　　❷ 风扇（　　）　　❸ 手套（　　）
　 灭火器（　　）　　　 照明（　　）　　　 事故（　　）

2. 把下列词语组合成短语或句子。Connect the words into phrases or sentences.

❶ ①按照　②要求　③安全　④严格　⑤必须

_____

❷ ①相应　②摆放　③位置　④灭火器　⑤在

_____

第35课 | 保养设备

3 ①安全   ②出现   ③事故   ④避免

_____

 热身 Warm-up

你认识这些词语吗？ Do you know these words?

图片	词语	英文
	yánjìn 严禁	strictly prohibit
	fěnchén 粉尘	dust
	yuánjiàn 元件	component
	gùzhàng 故障	failure
	yóuwū 油污	oil stain
	lǜwǎng 滤网	filter screen

337

 学习生词 **Words and Expressions**  35-01

1	保养	bǎoyǎng	*v.*	maintain
2	严禁	yánjìn	*v.*	strictly prohibit
3	及时	jíshí	*adv.*	timely
4	粉尘	fěnchén	*n.*	dust
5	进入	jìnrù	*v.*	enter
6	元件	yuánjiàn	*n.*	component
7	引起	yǐnqǐ	*v.*	cause
8	故障	gùzhàng	*n.*	failure
9	油污	yóuwū	*n.*	oil stain
10	污染	wūrǎn	*v.*	pollute
11	滤网	lǜwǎng	*n.*	filter screen
12	干净	gānjìng	*adj.*	clean
13	但是	dànshì	*conj.*	but
14	维修	wéixiū	*v.*	repair
15	解决	jiějué	*v.*	resolve, solve

第 35 课 | 保养设备

 词语练习 Word Exercises

1. 学习词语搭配。Study the collocations.

❶ bǎoyǎng 保养	bǎoyǎng shèbèi 保养 设备	maintain the equipment
	bǎoyǎng jīqì 保养 机器	maintain the machine
❷ jìnrù 进入	jìnrù diànnǎo 进入 电脑	enter the computer
	jìnrù yuánjiàn 进入 元件	enter the components
❸ gùzhàng 故障	yǐnqǐ gùzhàng 引起 故障	cause malfunction
	zhuāngbèi gùzhàng 装备 故障	equipment fault

2. 给词语选择正确搭配。Choose the right words to form collocations.

❶ _____ dǎkāi 打开　　A. yánjìn 严禁　　B. yuánjiàn 元件

❷ _____ qīnglǐ 清理　　A. jíshí 及时　　B. jìnrù 进入

❸ _____ gānjìng 干净　　A. qīnglǐ 清理　　B. jiějué 解决

339

学习课文 Text 🎧 35-02

1. 电气设备在工作的时候严禁打开。
2. 每次零件制作完成后,需要及时清理设备,防止粉尘进入电气元件内部,引起设备故障。
3. 各电气设备及元件还要防止油污等其他污染。
4. 各设备风扇的滤网要经常清洁,同时粉末要清理干净。
5. 工作缸无须保养,但是出现故障的时候,要及时维修解决。

第 35 课 | 保养设备

1. Opening electrical devices during their operation is strictly prohibited.
2. Each time after a part is completed, it is necessary to clean the devices timely to prevent dust from entering the electrical components and causing device failure.
3. All the electrical equipment and components should also be protected from oil stains and other contaminants.
4. The filter screens of the fans of all the devices should be cleaned regularly, and the powder should be removed thoroughly.
5. The working cylinder does not require maintenance, but when a failure occurs, it should be repaired and resolved timely.

课文练习 Text Exercises

1. 回答问题。Answer the questions.

① 各电气设备及元件要防止污染吗？

② 各设备的风扇的滤网要经常清洁吗？

2. 根据课文选词填空。Choose the words to fill in the blanks based on the text.

| A. 引起 | B. 进入 | C. 但是 | D. 污染 |

① 防止粉尘进入电气元件内部，_____设备故障。

② 工作缸无须保养，_____出现故障的时候，要及时维修解决。

学习语法 Grammar

 语法点 1　Grammar Point 1

代词"各"　The pronoun "各"

It is used before a noun or a measure word to indicate each individual in a large number of people or things.

1. 各电气设备及元件还要防止油污等其他污染。
2. 必须设定好各个参数。
3. 确保各设备运行正常。

选词填空。Choose the words to fill in the blanks.

| A. 各　　　　B. 都 |

1. _____电气设备及元件还要防止油污等其他污染。
2. 必须设定好_____个参数。
3. 检查一切_____正常后，按下"继续"按钮重新开始制造。
4. 三个打印参数_____设定好了。

语法点 2　Grammar Point 2

副词"经常"　The adverb "经常"

It is used before a verb to indicate high frequency.

1. 各设备风扇的滤网要经常清洁。
2. 经常使用的可黏合材料有金属、塑料等。
3. 在生物应用领域,经常使用的3D打印材料有人造骨粉、生物原料等。

选词填空。Choose the words to fill in the blanks.

A. 经常　　　　B. 比较

1. 各设备风扇的滤网要_____清洁。
2. 金属零件_____薄。
3. _____使用的可黏合材料有金属、塑料等。
4. 非金属零件_____软。

汉字书写　Writing Chinese Characters

rèn

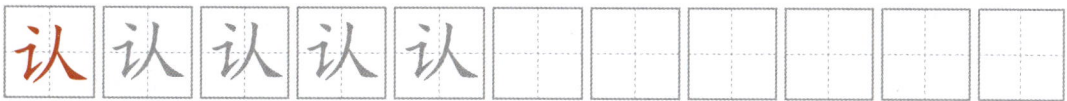

343

 文化拓展 Culture Insight

WeChat is a free application launched by Tencent in 2011, providing instant communication services for smart terminals. It enables the rapid sending of free voice messages, videos, images, and texts across networks, communication operators, and operating system platforms. Additionally, it offers services such as shared streaming media content and location-based social plug-ins. WeChat boasts over 1 billion monthly active users across more than 200 countries and regions and supports over 20 languages.

第35课 | 保养设备

 小结 Summary

1. 听句子选词填空。Listen to the sentences and choose the words to fill in the blanks. 🎧 35-03

> A. 引起　　　B. 滤网　　　C. 油污　　　D. 及时

① 每次零件制作完成后，需要_____清理设备。

② 防止粉尘进入电气元件内部，_____设备故障。

③ 各设备风扇的_____要经常清洁，同时粉末要清理干净。

④ 各电气设备及元件还要防止_____等其他污染。

2. 看词语练拼音。Look at the words and practice Pinyin.

| wéihù | yǐnqǐ | yuánjiàn | jīngcháng |
| 维护 | 引起 | 元件 | 经常 |

| diànjī | fēngshàn | lǜwǎng | bǎoyǎng |
| 电机 | 风扇 | 滤网 | 保养 |

3. 朗读下列句子。Read aloud the following sentences.

① Diànqì shèbèi zài gōngzuò de shíhou yánjìn dǎkāi.
电气设备在工作的时候严禁打开。

② Gōngzuògāng wúxū bǎoyǎng, dànshì chūxiàn gùzhàng de shíhou, yào jíshí wéixiū jiějué.
工作缸无须保养，但是出现故障的时候，要及时维修解决。

第36课 Lesson 36
Chǔlǐ gùzhàng
处理故障
Troubleshooting

 复习 Revision

1. 根据图片选择词语。Choose the words based on the pictures.

❶ 维修（　　）　　❷ 粉尘（　　）　　❸ 严禁（　　）
　故障（　　）　　　油污（　　）　　　网络（　　）

2. 把下列词语组合成短语或句子。Connect the words into phrases or sentences.

1 ①工作　②打开　③严禁　④时

_____

2 ①元件　②粉尘　③进入　④防止

_____

第36课 | 处理故障

3 ①清理　　②粉尘　　③干净　　④要

_____

热身 Warm-up

你认识这些词语吗？　Do you know these words?

	xùhào 序号	serial number
	cuòwù 错误	error, mistake
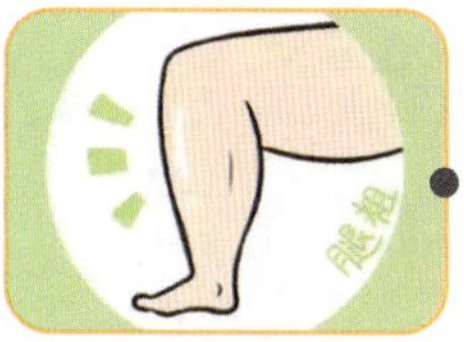	biàncū 变粗	thicken
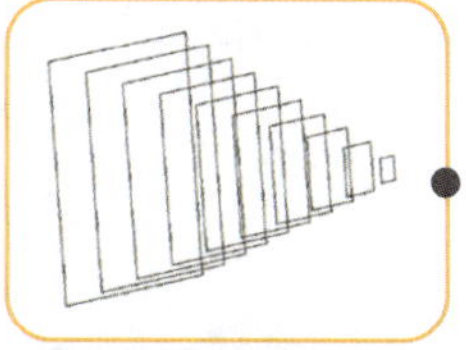	biànxiǎo 变小	get smaller
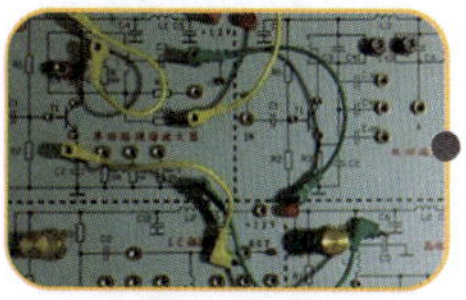	xiànlù 线路	circuit
	xiànwèi 限位	limit

学习生词 Words and Expressions  36-01

1	常见	cháng jiàn	*phr.*	common
2	产生	chǎnshēng	*v.*	occur
3	原因	yuányīn	*n.*	reason, cause
4	方法	fāngfǎ	*n.*	method
5	序号	xùhào	*n.*	serial number
6	错误	cuòwù	*n.*	error, mistake
7	变粗	biàncū	*phr.*	thicken
8	变小	biànxiǎo	*phr.*	get smaller
9	光路	guānglù	*n.*	optical path
10	偏移	piānyí	*v.*	offset, deviate
11	过高	guò gāo	*phr.*	ultra-high
12	线路	xiànlù	*n.*	circuit
13	损坏	sǔnhuài	*v.*	damage
14	限位	xiànwèi	*v.*	limit
15	更换	gēnghuàn	*v.*	replace

第 36 课 | 处理故障

词语练习 Word Exercises

1. 学习词语搭配。Study the collocations.

① chǎnshēng 产生	chǎnshēng yuányīn 产生　原因	cause of the occurrence
	chǎnshēng gùzhàng 产生　故障	cause of the malfunction
② guānglù 光路	tiáojié guānglù 调节　光路	adjust the optical path
	guānglù piānyí 光路　偏移	optical path offset
③ gēnghuàn 更换	gēnghuàn kāiguān 更换　开关	replace the switch
	gēnghuàn shèbèi 更换　设备	replace the equipment

2. 给词语选择正确搭配。Choose the right words to form collocations.

① _____ gùzhàng 故障　　A. cháng jiàn 常　见　　B. jìnrù 进入

② _____ yuányīn 原因　　A. chǎnshēng 产生　　B. jiǎnchá 检查

③ xiànlù 线路 _____　　A. jiějué 解决　　B. sǔnhuài 损坏

 学习课文 Text 36-02

常见故障、产生原因及解决方法如下：
Common faults, causes of the occurrences, and their solutions are as follows:

序号 No.	常见故障 Common faults	产生原因 Causes of the occurrences	解决方法 Solutions
1	图形文件异常 Abnormal graphic file	软件转换STL文件格式错误 Error in converting to the STL file format through the software	将模型文件通过软件重新转换 Reconvert the model file through the software
2	激光器扫描变粗、功率变小 Thickened scanning and reduced power of the laser	光路偏移 Optical path deviation	调节光路 Adjust the optical path

第 36 课 ｜ 处理故障

3	激光器不工作 jīguāngqì bù gōngzuò Laser not working	① 加载失败 jiāzài shībài Loading failed ② 温度过高 wēndù guò gāo Ultra-high temperature ③ 线路损坏 xiànlù sǔnhuài Circuit damage ④ 激光器损坏 jīguāngqì sǔnhuài Laser damage	① 重新加载 chóngxīn jiāzài Reload ② 检查冷却装置 jiǎnchá lěngquè zhuāngzhì Check the cooling device ③ 检查线路 jiǎnchá xiànlù Check the circuit ④ 检查激光器 jiǎnchá jīguāngqì Check the laser
4	限位故障 xiànwèi gùzhàng Limit fault	限位开关损坏 xiànwèi kāiguān sǔnhuài Limit switch damage	更换开关 gēnghuàn kāiguān Replace the switch

课文练习　Text Exercises

1. 回答问题。Answer the questions.

   ① 图形文件异常需要重新转换吗？
   ② 激光器扫描变粗是因为激光器损坏了吗？

2. 根据课文选词填空。Choose the words to fill in the blanks based on the text.

A. 线路　　　　B. 方法　　　　C. 偏移　　　　D. 变小

❶ 激光器扫描变粗、功率_____。
❷ 激光器_____损坏，需要检查线路。

学习语法 Grammar

语法点 1　Grammar Point 1

动词"如下"　The verb "如下"

It indicates being as listed or described below. The common structure is: noun + 如下, or verb + 如下 + noun.

❶ 常见故障、产生原因及解决方法如下。
❷ 模型打印需完成如下步骤。
❸ 3D 打印使用的打印材料如下。

选词填空。Choose the words to fill in the blanks.

A. 如下　　　　B. 例如

❶ 常见故障、产生原因及解决方法_____。
❷ 模型打印步骤_____。

3 可以通过获取被测物体表面大量密集的数据信息，_____三维坐标、纹理等，快速建立三维模型。

4 操作切片软件的时候，需要设定很多参数，_____层厚、壁厚等。

语法点 2　Grammar Point 2

副词"过"　The adverb "过"

It is used before an adjective to indicate an extreme or unreasonable degree.

1 温度过高。
2 液体高度过低。
3 水冷机控制温度过高。

选词填空。Choose the words to fill in the blanks.

A. 过　　　　B. 通过

1 温度_____高。
2 液体高度_____低。
3 可以_____添加支撑，防止模型发生变形。
4 还可以_____什么快速建立目标的三维模型？

 汉字书写 Writing Chinese Characters

 职业拓展 Career Insight

The main causes of abnormal heating of the 3D printer platform are problems with the thermistor or the heating block circuit. Use a multimeter to check whether the circuit is disconnected. If it is, replace the circuit. If there is no problem with the circuit, you need to check whether the interfaces at both ends of the circuit are loose. If they are, disassemble the

interfaces and reconnect them. If none of the above problems is found, the thermistor is probably damaged and needs to be replaced.

小结 Summary

1. 听句子选词填空。 Listen to the sentences and choose the words to fill in the blanks.  36-03

> A. 过高　　B. 原因　　C. 失败　　D. 常见

1 加载_____。

2 _____故障。

3 温度_____。

4 产生_____。

2. 看词语练拼音。 Look at the words and practice Pinyin.

| chǎnshēng | xùhào | guānglù | sǔnhuài |
| 产生 | 序号 | 光路 | 损坏 |

| piānyí | biàncū | xiànwèi | cháng jiàn |
| 偏移 | 变粗 | 限位 | 常见 |

3. 朗读下列句子。 Read aloud the following sentences.

1 Ruǎnjiàn zhuǎnhuàn STL wénjiàn géshi cuòwù.
软件 转换 STL 文件 格式 错误。

2 Jīguāngqì sǎomiáo biàncū, gōnglǜ biànxiǎo.
激光器 扫描 变粗，功率 变小。